The *Alef-Bet* of Death
Dying as a Jew

A Guide for the Dying out of Jewish Traditional Sources

RABBI ARIEL STONE

Copyright © 2019 Rabbi Ariel Stone.

All rights reserved. No part of this book may be reproduced, stored, or transmitted by any means—whether auditory, graphic, mechanical, or electronic—without written permission of the author, except in the case of brief excerpts used in critical articles and reviews. Unauthorized reproduction of any part of this work is illegal and is punishable by law.

All scripture are translated by the author from the original Hebrew Bible "Tanakh".

ISBN: 978-1-4834-9495-1 (sc)
ISBN: 978-1-4834-9497-5 (hc)
ISBN: 978-1-4834-9496-8 (e)

Library of Congress Control Number: 2018914593

Because of the dynamic nature of the Internet, any web addresses or links contained in this book may have changed since publication and may no longer be valid. The views expressed in this work are solely those of the author and do not necessarily reflect the views of the publisher, and the publisher hereby disclaims any responsibility for them.

Any people depicted in stock imagery provided by Getty Images are models, and such images are being used for illustrative purposes only.
Certain stock imagery © Getty Images.

Lulu Publishing Services rev. date: 01/25/2019

Two good things are near to you and far from you,
far from you and near to you:

Repentance is near to you and far from you,
far from you and near to you.

Death is near to you and far from you,
far from you and near to you.

—*Kohelet Rabbah* 8:17

ז״ל
In memory of all those who taught by the way
they died something important
that I, their witness and messenger, try to convey to the next deathbed,
among them
Rudette Muzzana, Cathy Thaler, Roz Levine,
Shirley Renner, Eileen Rose, and Lee Levy.

And in memory of my teacher
Dr. Byron Sherwin.

And especially for
Andy Hamon,
who started it all when he asked, "Where is
the book for me, I who am dying?"

זכרונם לברכה
Zikhronam l'vrakha,
the memory of their lives is a blessing in mine.

מי שאין לו מקום בשום מקום
יש לו מקום בכל מקום

mi sheh-ayn lo makom b'shum makom,
yesh lo makom b'kol Makom

Someone who has no place anywhere
finds a place in the Place that is all places.[1]

The Alef Bet of Death and its companion, *Dying as a Jew*, are for you if you have an awareness that you are going to die soon and if you, knowing yourself to be part of the people of Israel by birth or by choice, seek support and guidance from Jewish tradition to help you bear the burden of that knowledge. Dying is not a moment at the end of life; it is a path, and there are steps to take and choices to make as you walk that path.

That path may seem short or long as you gaze upon it from where you now stand. You may have been diagnosed with a terminal illness, or you may have been living with a chronic, slowly progressing condition that is now worsening, or you may be healthy yet now know with a painful clarity, for any reason whatsoever, that you will soon die.

This is not a book about science, although there is some science in it. It is not about belief, although there are beliefs and practices described.

This is not a book for mourners. There are a myriad of those.

This is a book for you as you face the path that leads to your death. It shares stories of those who have gone before you. It offers you ways to think and feel and wonder about your death. It is sometimes more poetic, sometimes more factual—not unlike your own frame of mind. Some days, you may be intensely interested in facts; on other days, you will be struck by the way a drop of dew glistens on a leaf.

You are dying. You will die.

Dying is natural. Your body knew right down to the miracle of your individual cells and their mysterious workings how to be born; it knew how to grow, and it knows how to die. The spirit may feel afraid of the dark. It may not realize that by its very nature it gives light. May this guide to dying help you see the light that you shed, step by step. May it illuminate the path before you. You too have something to teach in the way you die.

נר ה׳ נשמת אדם
ner HaShem nishmat adam
"The human soul is G*d's light."[2]

א	ALEF	The Letter *Alef* Has No Sound; There Are No Words
ב	BET	*Barukh Dayan ha-Emet,* Blessed Is the True Judge
ג	GIMMEL	*Gesisah,* the Last Phase of Dying
ד	DALET	*Da'avah,* Grief
ה	HEY	*Hester Panim,* the Hiding of the Face
ו	VAHV	*Vidui Sh'khiv MeyRa',* Confession of the Dying
ז	ZAYIN	*Zakhor,* Remember
ח	KHET	*Hesed v'Emet,* Steadfast Loyalty
ט	TET	*Tum'ah,* the Touch of Death
י	YUD	*Yir'ah Mipnei haMavet,* Fear of Death
כ	KAF	*Kavod haMeyt,* Honoring the Dead Body
ל	LAMED	*Levush,* Clothing
מ	MEM	*Mitzvah,* Sacred Obligation
נ	NUN	*Neshek,* Kiss or Armor; the Deathbed Blessing
ס	SAMEKH	*Sur MeyRa',* Turn Away from Evil
ע	AYIN	*Ayin*—Nothingness
פ	PEH	*Peh,* the Mouth of G*d
צ	TZADI	*Tzelem Elohim,* the Image of G*d
ק	KUF	*Kadosh*, Holy
ר	REYSH	*Refu'ah,* Healing
ש	SHIN	*Shaddai,* Shelter
ת	TAHV	*Tefilah,* Prayer

3

Contents

The Letter *Alef* Has No Sound; There Are No Words 6
Barukh Dayan ha-Emet, Blessed Is the True Judge 8
Gesisah, the Last Phase of Dying 10
Da'avah, Grief 12
Hester Panim, the Hiding of The Face 14
Vidui Sh'kiv MeyRa, Confession of the Dying 16
Zakhor, Remember 18
Hesed v'Emet, Steadfast Loyalty 20
Tum'ah, the Touch of Death 22
Yir'ah Mipnei haMavet, Fear of Death 24
Kavod haMeyt, Honoring the Dead Body 26
Levush, Clothing 28
Mitzvah, Sacred Obligation 30
Neshek, Kiss or Armor; the Deathbed Blessing 32
Sur MeyRa', Turn Away from Evil 34
Ayin—Nothingness 36
Peh, the Mouth of G*d 38
Tzelem Elohim, the Image of G*d 40
Kadosh, Holy 42
Refu'ah, Healing 44
Shaddai, Shelter 46
Tefilah, Prayer 48

Endnotes to Volume 1: The Alef Bet of Death 115

א
The Letter *Alef* Has No Sound; There Are No Words

The day on which you die, according to Jewish tradition, is your own private Yom Kippur. Why? Because contemplation of death by the living brings an agony of fear.

The ancient Jewish sages saw that the suffering this fear causes offers us a moral opportunity, so they taught us to understand death as a chance for a final moment of repentance. Judaism does not emphasize deathbed confession, but the sages knew, as you now do, that the approach of death clarifies the heart, and it often brings a sense of regret for that left undone and for those left distanced.

Why call it repentance? In the process of dying, you may find that your perspective on your life has been altered from the vibrant sense of yourself as the center of the universe. The dying can see the brevity of a life within the vast life of the universe. A sense of awe dawns for the great and mysterious oneness of which we are so small a part—but a grateful part nevertheless. We repent of the self-centered distraction separating us from that oneness.

> Rava said to Rav Nakhman, "Show yourself to me [in a dream after you die]." He showed himself to Rava. Rava asked him, "Was death painful?" Rav Nakhman replied, "It was as painless as lifting a hair from a cup of milk. But were the Holy Blessed One to say to me, 'You may return to that world where you were before,' I would not do it. The fear of death is too great."

> The Eternal fashioned the human being, *afar min ha-adamah,* dust from the earth, and breathed into its nostrils *nishmat hayim,* the breath of life.[3]

According to the ancient story, G*d shaped us of earth, *adamah*, and blew breath, *neshamah*, into us. We are a mixture of earth and heaven, of flesh and spirit, and of dust and dreams. The dust of which we are made—a myriad of tiny atomic particles—does not die. Only the temporary gathering of it into the form of you does. The substance of our physical lives is caught up in a universe-wide recycling. *Yashov he-afar al ha-aretz,* the dust returns to the earth, and *ha-ruakh tashuv el ha-Elohim,* "the breath returns to G*d."[4]

To repent in Jewish tradition is not to become new or different; it is *teshuvah*, return, to the innocent, pure clarity of being in which you began the journey of life. Dying is a return to the all of which we are a part—that place where words fail us and are, anyway, unnecessary. As you return to the presence, your consciousness goes where words, even as your body, cannot follow.

לך דומיה תהילה - *L'kha dumiyah tehilah*—to You, silence is praise.[5]

ב ברוך דין האמת

Barukh Dayan ha-Emet, Blessed Is the True Judge

When one hears of a death, the traditional Jewish response is the shortest of all Hebrew prayers: *barukh dayan ha'emet*. Its brevity conveys breathlessness, shock, and dismay—a quick gasp and an exclamation.

It is not an utterance of thanksgiving; it is an acceptance. This "judgment" is not meant personally; you are not being judged and punished. Rather, this prayer expresses recognition of the truth that there is a natural law of all life. *Barukh Dayan ha-Emet* expresses our awareness that death is not an unexpected end to life and love. It is a way of saying, "I rejoiced in life, and now I must accept that to everything there comes an end. It is *emet*, or truth."

An ancient teaching observes that the word *emet*, truth, is made up of letters located as far as possible from one another in the Hebrew *alef-bet*: first, middle, and last.[6] This symbolizes the all-embracing nature of truth. It demonstrates that truth may actually be composed of elements that seem very far from one another and may be, perhaps, even as contradictory as *alef* and *tav*, the beginning and the end of the *alef-bet*.

There is no blessing recorded for hearing of one's own impending death. There is much Jewish lore relating efforts to outsmart the messenger of death by changing a name or a place of residence. Other stories even encourage the belief that Torah study protects from death. Yet Torah, understood by our people as Jewish life wisdom, will teach us only how to die, not how to avoid death.

> Rabbi Akiba said: "what relevance does such a story have? The story is of no consequence to me … Consider

now: Moshe performed so many *mitzvot,* so many acts of *tzedakah.* Yet in the end he was told "the time draws near for you to die" (Deuteronomy 31:14). It's inevitable: there is "a time to be born, and a time to die" (Ecclesiastes 3:2).[7]

As it is said, no one's getting out of here alive. There is some consolation in knowing that this is a judgment upon us all and that there is love and support that will be offered—such precious blessings!—to each of us as we are walking through the valley. A midrash describes the final act of a life as the return of the borrowed soul to G*d. Life is the ultimate blessing. In our gratitude, we finally, ultimately, learn to respond by returning the blessing. Through our lives, we give life in ways we will never know.

גם כי אלך בגי צלמות לא אירה רע כי אתה עמדי
Even when I walk in the valley of the shadow of death,
I will be at peace,
for I know that I am part of the circle of life and death
embracing all the world.[8]

ג גסיסה
Gesisah, the Last Phase of Dying

The last step in the path from life to death is called *gessisah*; the one dying is called the *gosses*. Jewish law traditionally defines this time as three days—seventy-two hours.

In the Talmud, the principle is set forth that a dying person is *hai l'kol davar*, meaning that the person is "alive for all purposes"; such a person can still inherit and bestow, and in all ways, this person is to be respected as the person he or she has always been.

One must take great care in the treatment of someone in the state of gesisah.

> If in the vicinity there is something which delays the dying person's death, such as a woodchopper working outside, or salt on the *goses'* tongue, it is permitted to remove these obstacles to the soul's departure.[9]

In the past, our ancestors believed that the feathers in pillows caused an impediment to the dying process, so it became the custom in certain places to remove a person's pillow so as to help the dying process along. The great medieval commentator Rabbi Moshe Isserles explains that "it is prohibited to do that which prevents the dying person from dying quickly—anything which impedes the dying process may be removed. But to do that which will cause death more quickly is prohibited."[10]

Today it is very difficult to know when the dying process is impeded and when it is respected. There is a very fine line between medical therapies that support the health of a person who may be healed and those that are applied in a refusal to recognize, and respect, the natural process of dying.

Even more agonizing is the attempt to clearly see when the one has become the other. When is the choice of one more procedure a chance to live and be well again, and when is it only a way to hide from the reality that death is imminent?

> Against your will, you were formed; against your will, you were born; against your will, you live; against your will, you will die; against your will, you will give an accounting of your life.

One may do nothing to shorten life, for there is no command greater than *pikuakh nefesh*, the saving of life. One may do nothing to prolong dying, for "there is a time to live and a time to die," and to rebel against nature and the divine will is only destructive human hubris.

ד דאבה

Da'avah, Grief

Grief is a terrible suffering, and as we grieve for others' lives lost, surely we also grieve the loss of our own. The suffering of grief is not to be avoided, according to Jewish tradition. We are urged not to be afraid, though we walk in the valley of the shadow of death. But we are: we are terrified, and we do bargain, and perhaps we are angry. Midrash—traditional Jewish lore—reveals that our great ancestors, our teachers Moses and Aaron, were no different.

> When Rabbi Bunam lay dying, his wife burst into tears. He said, "What are you crying for? My whole life was only that I might learn how to die."

Yet suffering the grief of knowing the end of one's own life to be near also offers opportunity for vision. This is the truth within the simplistic assertion that everything happens for a reason: in every human experience, there is a chance to see, learn, and know something that otherwise would have been lost.

Contemplating an understanding that can be reached only on the other side of suffering, in 1908, Rabbi Yehudah Leib Alter of Ger considered a famous line from the Passover Haggadah:

It is written after the four expressions of redemption [I will *bring you out*, I will *deliver you*, I will *redeem you*, I will *take you to Me*] "and you will know that I am 'ה " (Shemot 6:7) which is the ultimate aim of redemption. For this they had to be in Egypt for four hundred years.[11]

In other words, it takes the entirety of a lifetime, with all its suffering, to see what is there to see and to know what we might come to know.

We cannot avoid the suffering of grief, and we should not try. When we meet the suffering that comes to us not as a blow but as the rung of a ladder, and when we grasp that ladder and hold on, then we will see. The ladder is the image the mystics offer you. Not every day will be a day for climbing it, they know that some days your spirit feels small and overwhelmed.

But other days will be graced by a good poem, a beautiful song, or an act of love, and on those days, your spirit will expand, and you will find the strength to rise upon that rung, not past your grief but through it and because of it. You will rise from seeing to learning and then, perhaps, to knowing something important. You may even achieve understanding. And in the end, you will feel yourself lifted above the suffering of grief, and you will know peace.

ה הסתר פנים

Hester Panim, the Hiding of The Face

Where is G*d in suffering? Where is G*d in the fear of death? During the Holocaust, Jews were faced with a murderous evil that caused some to wonder if G*d was no longer present among them; they spoke of the Jewish belief that "sufferings are *hester panim*, concealment of the Divine Face." Had G*d turned away from the Jews? Does G*d see our suffering? Rabbi Kalonymos Kalman Shapira, suffering in the Warsaw Ghetto along with his disciples, refused to support this kind of believing.

> When a person perceives within his suffering the Hand of G*d, and His justice and truth, he abolishes the *hester* (concealment). He reveals G*d even out of the *hester* and *dinim* (judgments). Then, as the concealment evaporates, it becomes *hesed* (loving-kindness), which reveals the Divine Light that is the Face of G*d.

*My heart says, seek Your face; Your face, O G*d, I long to see.*

Rabbi Shapira continued: In our suffering, we say that there is no G*d, for the human soul in pain turns inward, blinded to all but the need for consolation.

> How could we ever have said that the pain concealed G*d's Face? Not only does G*d say (Psalm 91:15) "I am in pain with him," but G*d, the blessed One, endures the brunt of our pain. On the contrary, it is the person who does not accept suffering with acquiescence, G*d forbid, and thinks that his suffering is unjustified, G*d forbid, who create the concealment. It is as if, G*d forbid, he was doing away with G*d, as it were.[12]

In suffering, you may believe that you are alone, but in truth, it is only that your eyes are closed in pain, and you can no longer see anything at all.

The first question asked of us by G*d in the Torah is *ayeka?* Where are you? On the spiritual path to death, you are able to see, for the first time, that the answer to the question is not a matter of your control, your agility, or your aptitude. It is only a matter of the distance between believing that one has an independent existence and understanding that one's existence is completely inseparable from the All of Life, which is called in Jewish tradition by the name of G*d. The path to death is exactly the distance between seeing the veil of day-to-day perceptions, in which you experience yourself as a separate individual, and peering behind that veil to the hidden, deeper truth. At the end of the path, one comes to understand that "all your strength and mind and independence is nothing but a piece of G*d in you."[13] And so we find it written that "Moses hid his face" (Exodus 3:6) because he came to the realization that all is G*d, and it was in comparison as if he, a simple individual human being, did not have a face of his own at all. What he did have, and always and forever would have, is a part of G*d's.

ו וִדּוּי שְׁכִיב מְרַע

Vidui Sh'kiv MeyRa, Confession of the Dying

This prayer is recited when you are ready to let go of life, or it is recited for you as you are dying.

My G*d, G*d of my fathers and my mothers, my prayer comes now before you, do not turn away from my plea. Cover me, protect me in my recognition Of all my sins that I have sinned from the beginning of my time until this day. I am ashamed and disappointed of my evil deeds. In foolishness I turned away from the path of good and of justice, and it wasn't worth it. I cannot place blame on You f or injustice in my life. I know the truth; I too have done wrong. What shall I say before You, who dwells on high; what story shall justify me before the All of heavens and of dust? Mystery and commonplace is revealed now. No more secrets, no more hiddenness now.	אלהי ואלהי אבותי ואמותי תבוא לפניך תפילתי ואל תתעלם מתחינתי ותכפר לי על כל חטאתי שחטאתי לפניך מעודי על היום הזה בושתי וגם נכלמתי ממעשי הרעים הסכלתי כי עשיתים סרתי ממצותיך וממשפטיך הטובים ולא שוה לי ואתה צדיק על כל הבא עלי כי אמת עשית ואני הרשעתי מה אומר לפניך יושב מרום ומה אספר לפניך שוכן שחקים? הלא כל הנסתרות והנגלות אתה יודע אתה יודע רזי עולם ותעלומות סתרי כל חי אתה חופש כל חדרי בטן ובוחן כליות ולב אין דבר נעלם ממך ואין נסתר מנגד עיניך ובכן יהי רצון מלפניך ה' אלהי ואלהי אבותי ואמותי שתסלח לי על כל חטאתי ותמחול לי על כל עונותי ותכפר לי על כל פשעי מגן יתומים ודין שכולים רחם על קרובי היקרים היה להם למחסה חלצם מכל צרה והנחם בדרך ישרה המודה אני לפניך ה' אלהי ואלהי אבותי ואמותי שעתותי בידך על כן בידך אפקיד רוחי פדית אותי ה' אל אמת ברוך אתה ה' אדון הרחמים והסליחות

In my bones I know it.
There is nothing that is hidden from
Your sight.
O let it be Your will,
HaShem my G*d and G*d of my
fathers and my
mothers, to forgive all my mistakes,
to erase all my
errors, and to cover me from all my
sins.
Shield of orphans, Judge of the
bereaved,
shelter my dear ones in endless
compassion.
Extricate them from grief,
console them with a clear path.
My timing now is in Your hands,
HaShem my G*d and G*d of my
fathers and my
mothers,
I know it; I entrust my spirit to You.
Take note of me, HaShem G*d of
Truth.
Blessed is HaShem,
Source of Compassion and
Forgiveness

ז זכור

Zakhor, Remember

In his book *Zakhor,* the historian Yosef Hayim Yerushalmi wrote that "what is remembered is not always recorded, and … much of what has been recorded is not necessarily remembered."[14]

Memory is a creation made of many parts, balanced between pain and compassion, haunted by longing. What we remember shapes what we become. Remembering is a *mitzvah,* a religious obligation, for Jews; it suffuses Jewish identity and community. Jews are to remember creation and the Exodus from Egypt with every Shabbat prayer and every kiddush over wine. Remembering, Judaism asserts, is a holy act.

We are taught that each of us is a reflection of G*d. That does not mean that we look, physically, like G*d. What we "see," in the reflection that is each of us, is not carried on the wavelength of visible light. It is memory that communicates the resemblance between Creator and creation. Memory is not a personal reverie; it is a collective, pulsing river of light, carrying the story of who we are, back and forth, all life long, creating us and forming G*d. Each individual's memory illuminates a small part of the darkness that surrounds us. In so doing, it reveals our memory of who we were and who we are together, because each of us was.

You are remembered through the influence you have upon others. Everyone living today does certain things, acts in certain ways, and cares about certain ideals, because of impressions made by others they will never forget, and by others they never knew, even years and years after the death of the one who created the memory.

> We do not need to build monuments for the righteous; their words and acts will be their memorial.

Curiously, we are also commanded to forget. Sometimes in the course of the ebb and flow of relationships, forgetting—letting something go—is the wisest act.

The memories that survive settle into the hearts of those whose lives bear the impact of yours. Those memories build a bridge that spans the abyss separating the living from the dead. In the Jewish rituals of *yahrzeit* and of *yizkor*, those who love you may light a candle for you. They may also give *tzedakah* in your memory, in honor of causes you care about, or that express the way you blessed the world in your life.

זכר צדיק לברכה
Zekher Tzaddik L'vrakha
The memory of a righteous person is a blessing.

ח חסד ואמת

Hesed v'Emet, Steadfast Loyalty

The term *hesed v'emet* can be translated "mercy and truth," qualities that are also implicit in the idea of unwavering loyalty. The sages of ancient Israel wondered what it might mean to be that dependable in support of a dying person.

> When he was dying, our ancestor Jacob asked his children to "deal with me with *hesed v'emet*, 'mercy and truth'." The Sages interpret: "if you do *hesed* for me after my death, that is *hesed shel emet*, a true steadfast loyalty."[15]

The rabbis teach that *hesed shel emet* is caring for those who are unable to return the kindness. This kindness is offered without expectation of reward or repayment—for the dead cannot bury themselves, nor can they express gratitude for those who care for them. Long ago, the Jewish people created the *hevra kadisha*, "holy companions" who carry out this mitzvah and enable others to join them—steadfastly, reliably, faithfully. And in every Jewish community worthy of the name, no Jew goes without a dignified, simple Jewish burial, regardless of that Jew's means.

And so *hesed shel emet* comes to mean all that Jews do for each other around death.

We will fulfill the mitzvah of *shemirah*, "guarding": we will stay with your body when it is newly dead.

A *shomeyr*, a "guardian," will sit with you, reciting psalms and keeping a candle lit at your head and feet.

The *hevra kadisha* will wash your dead body, now called a *meyt* (male), *meytah* (female), or other terminology as may be appropriate,[16] and prepare it for burial. They will clothe it carefully while reciting psalms and prayers. This is called *taharah*, caring for a body that used to house a Jewish soul, in preparation for burial.

We will fulfill the final mitzvah, that of *halvayat hameyt*, "accompanying the dead." We will go with what is left of you, your body, to the cemetery, reciting more psalms and prayers and telling stories of your life, beginning our exploration of your legacy—that is, what your life will continue to mean to us.

We will not leave you alone until you are safely tucked into the embrace of your mother, the earth. And we will not forget you. You can rely upon it.

> The time drew near for Israel to die, and he called to his son Joseph and said, "If I have found favor in your eyes, please swear to me that you will deal with me with *hesed v'emet*, steadfast loyalty, and do not bury me in Egypt."

ט טומאה

Tum'ah, the Touch of Death

One who touches the dead, any dead body, is *tame'*.[17]

Ancient Israelites saw their safety in order. According to the account at the beginning of the Torah, first there was chaos, which became creation when G*d imposed order upon it. Light follows darkness in regular progression; water and dry land and air all have a place; all creatures participate in a living web that depends upon a complex order of interaction. In the Torah, even the Israelites camping in the wilderness set their tents in careful order.

That which cannot be ordered, or which becomes disordered, upends the sense of control that order offers. Naturally occurring transitions, such as that from life to death, cannot be ordered and cannot be controlled. This is one way of understanding the concept of *tum'ah*, "ritual impurity."

Death is the most powerful tum'ah, the most disordering, that the living can know. One who comes into contact with it is changed powerfully, and so Judaism teaches that one who has been so touched by this tum'ah must pause, drop out of ordinary activities of life, and take time to move through the disordering of all that seemed orderly.

To be in the presence of death disorders one. As this is true for those who gather around you, how much more so is it true for you. As you die, your self begins to "dis-order." You are no longer entirely of this world. You may find yourself reordering your priorities, even as the order of your days changes, shifts, or disappears completely. You cannot control this.

The molecules of your very being are beginning to spread out beyond your physical body, from your soul and from your emotional and mental being. Your physical body will follow.

As you follow the path of dying, there is a very slow dissolution of the candle flame of your being into the light around you. You are no longer so separate from the people on the sidewalk beyond your window, the rain bathing the garden, the trees and the sky and the earth around you. This is the beauty that lies beyond the fear of disorder; only here can you see that all that seemed separate now merges into one.

This light by which you are now beginning to see that all is one was created, according to Jewish mystical teachings, on the first day. "The light created by the blessed Holy One in the act of Creation flared from one end of the universe to the other, and was hidden away." It has been waiting for you until the day when, for you, "the worlds will be fragrant and all will be One."[18]

י ירָאָה מִפְּנֵי הַמָּוֶת
Yir'ah Mipnei haMavet, Fear of Death

Fear is the natural response of the living to the approach of death. But fear belongs only to the land of the living; you will leave it behind at the right time. In ancient Jewish tradition, leaving the solid earth under our feet for the uncertain footing of floating at sea hints at experiences that those standing on solid ground can never understand or share.[19] It is only in dying, we are taught, that we will see what we have never been able to see before.

> "No one can see Me and live" (Exodus 33:20)—in one's lifetime one cannot; in one's death, one can.[20]

As you die, you will begin to feel less of this world. Your you-ness, your self, your soul, the very essence of you, will begin to cross over from the realm of life to that of death.

You float, balanced between here and not-here, for a time. You think many thoughts and feel many emotions. You remember much and regret some of those memories, but you also remember beautiful, wondrous moments.

Then your balance shifts, and the hold of your emotions begins to ease. Fear, anger, and pain belong to life and the living; these emotions are useful tools that help the living to live. But they are not necessary in death, and they will not be with you now.

Within the darkness, there will be light, not the light of a lamp but the brilliance of the presence of eternity. It will be visible to you not with your eyes but with your soul. As the light of your soul moves toward its Source, you will no longer feel pain, and you will leave anger behind.

You will no longer know fear. As your light merges with that eternal light, you will gently, quietly, peacefully become one with it, your consciousness growing wider and broader, stretching into translucence, disappearing into the endless flow of all that is.

בידו אפקיד רוחי בעת אישן ואעירה ועם רוחי גויתי ה' לי ולא אירא
B'yado afkid rukhi b'eyt ishan v'ah-ira, v'im rukhi, g'viyati, HaShem li v'lo ira

In G*d's hand I entrust my soul when I sleep and when I wake
And with my soul, my body—G*d is with me, I will not fear.[21]

כ כבוד המת

Kavod haMeyt, Honoring the Dead Body

Kavod hameyt, "the honor of the dead body," is an essential principle of Jewish ethics. Respectful treatment of a dead human being concludes with burial in a plain wooden casket in a plain shroud, and a simple grave marker.

Jewish tradition asserts that death is not the time to display economic status, nor to try to avoid the painful truth of death with "lifelike" viewings, or by delaying the funeral longer than absolutely necessary due to Shabbat, or a holy day. When families and friends are distant, we wait long enough to allow loved ones to gather and, if called for, for the mitzvah of organ donation to be fulfilled.

> These are the days of the years of Abraham's life; he lived 175 years. Abraham expired, and died in a good old age, an old man, and full of years; and was gathered to his people. Isaac and Ishmael his sons buried him in the cave of *Makhpelah*, in the field ... which is before Mamre ... there was Abraham buried, and Sarah his wife.[22]

Jewish tradition holds that Isaac, Rebekah, Jacob, and Leah are also buried in that family cave. In ancient Israel, a stone would be rolled over the cave's entrance, and a year later, the bones of the most recent dead would be added to a family receptacle. Thus you would literally be "gathered to your ancestors." In exile, Jews began to bury in the ground. While there is no specific commandment that requires burying one's whole body in the ground, the practice of cremation became anathema for many Jews, either as a form of

Rav Sheshet saw the angel of death in the marketplace. He said, "Do you want to take me here in the marketplace, like an animal? Come home with me!"

disrespect to the body or because so many murdered were cremated during the Holocaust.

Today, many Diaspora Jewish families are far-flung, and sometimes there is no one place in which it makes sense to establish a family cemetery plot. Some pay for their bodies to be buried in the Jewish homeland. Others are attracted to what seems to be the simplicity of cremation, despite the significant carbon footprint created by the intense heat needed to burn a human body. Green burial, in any place where a Jewish cemetery exists, is actually very close to Jewish traditional burial customs.

What is the best way to observe the mitzvah of *kavod hameyt* in burial today, in the twenty-first century? Perhaps there is no one answer. Yet there is a light that can be brought to bear from the Jewish ethics that guide Jewish dying with compassion.

ל לבוש

Levush, Clothing

A human body that is traditionally buried is covered in simple linen *takhrikhim,* "shrouds," by the *hevra kadisha* who prepare it for burial. This covering dates to the Second Temple period. Some also choose to be buried in a tallit.

But what does the soul wear? During your lifetime, it is clothed with your body—the body that weighs you down with its desires and urges and weaknesses. Yet like a good cloak in wintertime, the body also offers the soul protective cover. During life, the body is the vehicle of the soul's journey. Jewish mystical teachings describe the soul, as it leaves the body, clothed by a robe made of the acts of its life.

> Come and see: of Abraham, who was virtuous, what is written? *Ba bayamim,* "coming into days."[23] When he departed this world, he entered his very own days, clothing himself in them. Nothing was lacking from that garment of glory … happy are the righteous, whose days are pure and endure until the world that is coming! When they depart, they all conjoin and are woven into a garment of glory.[24]

The Zohar offers this interpretation of the ancient Hebrew idiom used to describe Abraham's death. *Ba bayamim* usually means "advanced in days," but the text, translating the phrase literally, uncovers a truth: when we die, the memory of how we used our days defines our character even as, in life, one's choice of clothing is often an overt statement of the way one seeks to be perceived in the world.

When you are dying, those around you will cover you with blankets to ward off the chill as your body's ability to maintain warmth declines. In death, we are "covered" by our acts. In ancient Hebrew, the word "cover," *kapporet,* means "hide." The rabbis wove the link to the word *kippur,* "atonement." Each of our acts is a thread in the weaving of our lives. By our own hands, we create the protective garment that covers us as we make our way forward into the unknown.

Some Jewish burial rites conclude with these last words spoken to the soul at the grave:

לך כי שלחל ה'
Lekh, ki shilakh'kha Yah
Go your way, for G*d has called you

לך וה' יהיה אמך
Lekh, vaYah yiheyeh imakh
Go your way, and may G*d be with you

והלך לפניך צדקך כבוד ה' יאספך
V'halakh l'fanekha tzidkekha, k'vod HaShem ya'asfekha
May your acts of justice go before you and the glory of G*d receive you

מ מצוה

Mitzvah, Sacred Obligation

> The Rabbis said to Rav Hamnuna Zuti at the wedding of Mar the son of Ravina, "sing for us!"
> He sang, "Woe for us that we are to die!"
> They said to him, "what shall we respond?"
> He sang, "Where is the Torah and the *Mitzvah* that will protect us?"[25]

The *mitzvah* of learning is central to Jewish life. The obligation to immerse yourself in study of that which is important, of good learning and careful thinking, supports your life, helping you choose your acts with a sense of the larger ethical impact of your life in the world. Good learning—insights, "aha!" moments, and reassurances about those questions that never get answered—also stays with you and helps you when you are dying.

> When you die, silver and gold and jewels do not accompany you. Only Torah-knowledge and *mitzvot* go along, as the verse says: "when you walk, it will guide you; when you lie down, it will watch over you (Proverbs 6:22). "When you walk, it will guide you" in this world; "when you lie down, it will watch over you" in the grave.[26]

Rabbi Yossi said, "May I be privileged to be among those who die in the midst of performing a *mitzvah.*"

Learning is a sacred obligation you owe to yourself and to all the rest of us, for it benefits not only you but the world you have touched and blessed with your life's actions.

This obligation is expressed with the word *mitzvah*. Often translated "command" or "good deed," it is, at its essence, a way of articulating a most elemental human need: a grateful response for the gift of life. The *mitzvot* (plural) are a system of acts meant to "give back" or "pay it forward"; this is easy to see in those that mandate acts of social kindness or economic justice. But every mitzvah is a key to something deeper still. Aware of one's life as a constant opportunity to do a mitzvah, the Jew's existential state is not "What do I deserve?" but rather "What is my obligation?"

It is taught: You were created unique; no other human being has ever existed or will ever exist that will be just like you. And there is a particular *mitzvah* that you are meant to do and that only you can do; there is a specific repair of this world that only you can achieve through the *mitzvah* you fulfill.

You cannot know which of the *mitzvot* is *the one* that manifests the difference your presence has made in the world. They all keep you company, and one of them is your destiny.

ב נשק

Neshek, Kiss or Armor; the Deathbed Blessing

There may be a moment when those who love you gather around you as you are dying, looking for some meaningful word. The Torah relates the mixed blessing that ensued when the patriarch Jacob summoned his children to his deathbed.

> Gather yourselves together and I will tell you what will happen to you in the End of Days. Assemble yourselves and listen, o children of Jacob; listen to Israel your father.[27]

Jacob did not know how to begin but began anyway. In his opening words, we can hear what he wanted to say. He wanted his children to stay together, to remain an "assembly" that listened to their parents and together carried on the meaning of their lives. The dying man begins to speak, and his opening words are not pleasant, but they are honest. He gives voice in these moments to that which usually goes unspoken, too difficult to say. It's not easy: at one point he cries out, "O G*d, I wait for your salvation!"[28]

"G*d, you are the strength of my salvation; you protect my head on the day of *neshek*" (Psalm 140:8) (this word can be translated as "kiss" or "armor," a reference to "armed battle").

The deathbed moment in Jewish tradition may occur long before the moment of death. It is a moment of recognizing, or avoiding, the relationships that matter. You choose the *neshek*: will your life end with armor or a kiss? Will you and those around you shrink away from the risks of honesty and openness and keep your emotional armor strong? Or will you manage to reach through the patterns and the fear, toward the closeness of the kiss?

> Jacob wished to bless his children, but was in doubt whether he ought to bless them since they had caused him so much pain … He turned his eyes and heart heavenwards, and cried out whatever G*d would put in his mouth to say.[29]

Those who are waiting find death most difficult. One may wait a lifetime to hear "I love you"; one never did ask about a long-ago heartache, because it was too painful to bring up, and so the ache remains. There is hesitation on both sides, and why, anyway, expect the pattern of a lifetime to be overcome now, just because death is near? Jacob speaks to each of his children of the choices that have already defined their lives, for good or for ill. There is no guarantee that deathbed honesty will change a life. But at the very least, Jacob's gift to his children meant that they were not left to wonder, all their lives long, what their father might have said.

ס סור מרע

Sur MeyRa', Turn Away from Evil

In the final moments before death, Jewish tradition provides for the recitation of the *Vidui Sh'kheyv MeyRa,* the final formal confession on the deathbed. It gives expression to the sense of regret we feel for that which is left undone, and more, that which we only wish we had left undone.

Jewish teaching regarding human sin and error paints for us a picture of a path upon which we walk all our days. The Hebrew word for our progress on that path is *halakha,* a "going" or "walking." The term *halakhah,* mistranslated as "law," speaks of guidance for walking the path of life. Mitzvah is the obligatory act that keeps one's feet—and heart—firmly upon the path.

There are those for whom the ethical behavior required seems easy; the path is wide and comfortable, with plenty of room for one's personal gait. Then there are those for whom the path seems narrow and restrictive, and they turn from it and even leave the path completely. This is natural human behavior, and for that reason, there are many teachings about turning away from one's temporary tangent and back toward the true path.

The ancient teaching sounds across the ages:

מי האיש החפץ חיים אוהב ימים לראות טוב
נצור לשונך מרע ושפתיה מדבר מרמה סור מרע עשה טוב בקש שלום ורודפהו

> You who desire life, and love good days, keep your tongue
> from evil and your lips from falsehood; *sur me'ra,* "turn away
> from evil" and do good; seek peace and pursue it.[30]

In the *Vidui,* we confess that we have "turned away" from the good path, and it has not availed us. It is difficult to face that confession, and there are those who object that a dying person should not be made to feel badly about past history. But as we have seen, Jewish tradition does not condescend to the dying, treating you as less than human; rather, you are *k'khai l'kol davar,* "a living person for every purpose" for as long as you are alive. And on any day, you can turn back to the right way in *teshuvah,* "turning."

Teshuvah is dependent upon nothing but a person's true regret and desire to turn. One's *teshuvah* does not have to be accepted by others in order to be valid. It only has to be real to you. You will know where you stand by the view:

> Rabbi Abbahu said, In the high place where the truly penitent stands, even the wholly righteous cannot stand.[31]

ע עִין

Ayin—Nothingness

At the beginning, there is nothing, and at the end, there is nothing, but this nothingness is not empty; it is made up of all that there is.

Ayin is a nothingness that is not empty but full of all that is not yet, that which always has been, and that which will continue to be, always.

We are all created of the same stuff that makes up the river of the universe. Although each of us is created unique on the level of human life, beneath the veil of daily life there is that which we all share. The true nature of our existence is that we are all part of an eternal flowing, and each of us a drop, special and unique, yet sharing an essential likeness with all those others that share in the flow within which we have our being.

> There is nothing, not even the smallest thing in the word, which is not held fast by its nature to the chain of existence; everything is a link in that chain, and is held fast by the power of its unity ... It is all one, without separation in its essential being.[32]

One of the Jewish names for G*d is Eternity of Time and Space. G*d is always, and for this short moment, you exist on that continuum; G*d is everywhere, and in this small space, you are here. You seem, to you and to us, to be crossing over from life to death. But the Jewish mystics understand that all being, and all movement, takes place within this one river of eternity.

You crossed from nothing into being, and now you will make that same crossing over, from being into nothing—no thing, no one thing, because you are becoming part of all that is. No more differentiation; it gives way to the no-thing-ness that is the true state of existence.

Before you were born, you are not here.
There is only what might be.
At the moment of birth, you cross over from oneness into existence.

After you die, you are not here.
There is only memory of what has been.
At the moment of death, we cross over from existence into oneness.

And the river of eternity flows on.

כ פֿה

Peh, the Mouth of G*d

G*d breathed into [the human] mouth *nishmat hayim*, the "breath of life."[33]

Our individual breathing life is part of the eternal living breath of the world. Life begins with the gift from eternity of the first breath; death is signaled by the last. The breath that was a moment ago within the body returns to the eternal cycle of breaths and breezes, winds and whining, singing, shouting, sighing. Even as G*d breathed the first breath into the first human, in a good death, G*d kisses away the last breath. The great mystic Maimonides describes the experience:

> Moses, the servant of G*d, died there in the land of Moab, *al peh*, by the mouth of, G*d. (Deuteronomy 34:5)

> The more one's forces of the body are weakened, and the fire of passion quenched, in the same measure does the mind increase in strength and light; knowledge becomes purer, and one is happy with one's knowledge. When this one is near death, knowledge mightily increases, joy in that knowledge grows greater, and love for the object of the knowledge grows more intense, and it is in this great delight that the soul separates from the body. To this state our Sages referred, when in reference to the death of Moses, Aaron and Miriam they said that death was in these three cases nothing but a kiss … the meaning of this saying ["by the mouth of G*d"] is that these three died in the mist of the pleasure derived from the knowledge of G*d and their great love for G*d …" Let him kiss me with the kisses of his mouth." (Song of Songs 1:2)[34]

In Hebrew, the word for breath, *neshimah,* is one small sound away from the word for soul, *neshamah.* To take time to breathe is, in a way, to recall one's soul and one's existence. In the Jewish prayer book, we are offered these ancient words composed by the rabbis of the Talmudic era two millennia ago. Praying Jews recite them every morning:

> My G*d, the *neshamah* that you have given me is pure. You created and formed it and breathed it into me, and one day you will take it from me, to return it to me in the future that is to come. All the time that my soul is within me I am thankful, my G*d and G*d of my fathers and mothers. You are the power in all life, seen and unseen. Blessed is the Source of Life for my soul.[35]

צ צלם אלקים

Tzelem Elohim, the Image of G*d

The creation of the human being is described in Genesis in this way: "G*d created the earthling in G*d's image: in the image of G*d they were created, male and female they were created."[36]

Like all of us, yet paradoxically absolutely uniquely, you are created in the image of G*d. For the rabbis of the Talmud, this means that you are possessed of infinite worth. When you die, a unique world—of potential, of possibility—dies.

> "And I will glorify G*d" means "be like G*d"—just as G*d is gracious and compassionate, so, too, should you be gracious and compassionate.[37]

The mystics asked: What does it mean to reflect G*d? What are we reflecting, and where? Might our acts in imitation of G*d bring G*d and goodness and blessing and light more fully into the world? Will our joy in life always be made bittersweet by our knowledge that we human beings are capable of both creating and destroying?

One who brings joy to the hearts of the disadvantaged resembles G*d, as the verse states, "Reviving the spirits of the lowly, reviving the hearts of the disadvantaged."

Rabbi Nahman of Bratslav taught by way of a parable: you are a unique portrait of the King, and the work of your life is this commission you received, by the fact of your birth, to create that portrait which is your unique image of G*d. To be created in that image and to know it is to struggle each day to know yourself and to become better at being yourself, for in so doing, you reflect the image in which you've been created ever more clearly.

This work is never completed while we are alive, for each day of life is one more day to understand—to add a color, or erase a line, or change a perspective. The creation of the painting is the journey of a lifetime, and it is only on the day of death—not one day earlier—that we each bring our completed portrait of the King, as it were, to the King.

> What are we human beings?
> What are we, that our existence might be noted in the cosmos?
> The breath is ephemeral, the heartbeat one note
> in the symphony of a vast and noisy universe.
> We are like grass, here and then gone, and only dust remains.
> Where is the wisdom that understands what it means to be mortal?
> …Teach us to count our days that we might open our hearts to wisdom.[38]

ק קדוש

Kadosh, Holy

"You shall be holy as I ה your G*d am Holy."[39]

We human beings are not intrinsically holy, according to Jewish teaching, but as images of the holy G*d, we are meant to become holy.

It is through, not despite, our everyday, simple human acts—in the messy, barely aware midst of each other—that we become holy. The regular words of the Jewish blessing—*asher kid'shanu b'mitzvotav*—assert that G*d "makes us holy through [the doing of] *mitzvot*."

> One does not approach the divine by reaching beyond the human but rather by becoming human.

The sense of the Hebrew *kadosh* means "setting apart." It's a paradox: the holy is that which is not part of our normal day-to-day, and yet we must seek it exactly there. The holy stands outside and apart, and yet we find it within and learn to see that it is a part of us.

The ancient Israelite priest was once designated to stand on the threshhold between the holy and the potentially holy, and to guide the average Israelite in approaching the holy. Since the destruction of the Jerusalem Temple put an end to sacrifice, there is very little for a priest to do in the formal sense.

But there is this: As you approach the transition between life and death in your dying, as you become less part of this world and more part of the all, as you rise past the self, you near that threshold; you become a priest to us. You become less like us living humans, and you become more like that which your essence reflects: the All that we call G*d.

How could it possibly occur to anyone to think that one might be holy like G*d? The Scriptures hint at it: another name for Holiness is Wisdom. It is written "Israel is holy to G*d, set apart as the first fruits of the harvest." (Jeremiah 2:3) As it is known, the word *B'reyshit* means "with the beginning", and as the mystics have revealed, *reyshit*[40] is Wisdom … one must try to reflect G*d in this, and undertake all one's acts *B'reyshit,* with Wisdom.[41]

In dying, you see what those who dwell in the land of the living cannot. Perhaps, as the mystics surmise, you may come to see the wisdom, the meaning, of the beginning of your life in its end. There is no human wisdom greater than to finally see what Isaiah saw:

Holy, holy, holy!—All the whole world is full of the glory of G*d![42]

ר רפואה

Refu'ah, Healing

We are created to live, and for the living, the prospect of death is terrifying. So much of our lives and our wherewithal are spent seeking that which keeps us healthy and that which will heal us when we are ill. As long as there is hope of life, thoughts of death are kept at bay.

A health care professional who cares for you may be respectful of the divine natural process of dying, yet, as a healer, still feels the impulse to try to fend off death. An example of this is seen in a story about the Baal Shem Tov (known as "the Besht"), a rabbi who was also a healer. A Rabbi Leibush, taken ill, had come to visit him, seeking a cure, and the Besht was working to heal him. Despite all the Besht's care, it happened that one day Rabbi Leibush took a turn for the worse. The Besht was in the study house when he was told, and he quickly ended his teaching.

> He hurried home and found the Angel of Death at the head of the bed. The Besht scolded the Angel of Death severely, and he ran away. The Besht then held Rabbi Leibush by the hand and he recovered immediately. He led him to the study hall,[43] as he was afraid to leave him at home lest the Angel of Death return, G*d forbid. After that the Besht said that because of what happened they wanted to reject him from both this world and the next world. He said that he did it only because it had happened so quickly. He had not seen any signs of death earlier. "When I saw the Angel of Death I suddenly felt grief-stricken and I acted."[44]

When you have crossed over into the place beyond fear, you are able to contemplate your death as a natural next step. But those around you, even those whom you most respect, may not be ready. They may take ill-advised steps in their panic.

This is your path; no one else can walk it or even see it clearly. The Jewish religious imperative is to respect the process of life and death as it naturally flows. Jewish law and ethics asserts that it is wrong to obstruct the peaceful progress of your death. Yes, life and its preservation is a sacred duty; *pikuah nefesh*, the "saving of a life," supersedes all other *mitzvot*. But the question remains: what is a meaningful definition of "life"? When is medical action no longer "saving"? When is "healing" a wholeness that is brought only by the peace of death?

> An old woman came before Rabbi Yose ben Halafta and said: "Master, I have grown so very old that my life has become hideous. I find no taste in food or drink, and I wish to depart from the world." He asked, "how did you extend your life so long?" She replied, "Whenever I have something to do, however enjoyable it may be, I am in the habit of putting it aside early every morning and going to the synagogue. He said, "for three days, one after another, keep yourself away from the synagogue." She went off and did as he advised, and on the third day she took sick and died.[45]

ש שדי

Shaddai, Shelter

> Imagine that you are in the middle of the sea, with a storm raging to the very heart of the heavens. You are hanging on by a hairsbreadth, not knowing what to do. You do not even have time to cry out. You can only lift your eyes and heart to G*d. You should always lift your heart to G*d like this. Seclude yourself and cry out to G*d. The danger is more than imaginary. As you know deep down in your soul, every person is in great danger in this world. Understand these words well.[46]

The all-encompassing waters from which you came, and to which you will return, are not always a calm, welcoming bath. The image of drowning conveys the terror of nonexistence in ancient Jewish writings. A Jew terrified by a void, watery or otherwise, might call upon *El Shaddai,* a name of G*d often associated with protectiveness.

No one knows precisely what *Shaddai* means. It is often translated "Almighty." It is also possible that it refers to the breast—G*d's breast; this motherly image is often associated with G*d's compassionate embrace. When we are most frightened, we want Mommy—not, perhaps, one's actual mother but the idealized image of the warm, soft, safe embrace protecting us from all harm, as it did in our youngest, earliest memory. The psalmist offers a metaphorical image of G*d as a large and powerful mother bird sheltering her young.

> One who dwells in the shelter of the Most High
> in the shadow of *Shaddai* at night
> I say of G*d, "My refuge and my safety, G*d in whom I trust
> … with pinions you are sheltered

> beneath wings you will take refuge
> this truth is your shield and your protection.[47]

On the *mezuzah* found on a Jew's door, there is often a visible letter *shin*. It stands, perhaps, for the first letter of the *Shema,* which is written within. Or perhaps it is meant to invoke that same protective sense of *Shaddai* at the doorway when we go out and when we come in.

The sense of the abyss can be encountered anywhere, but it is especially frightening to stand on a threshold between the place where one finds oneself and the place to which one is going when that place is entirely unknowable. The mezuzah on the doorpost blesses the passing through that liminal moment with the reminder that you are not alone.

לתקן עולם במלכות שדי

l'taken olam b'malkhut Shaddai

That which is hidden from our sight is whole in G*d's embrace

ת תפליה
Tefilah, Prayer

לך כי שלחך ה'
Go, for G*d is sending for you.
לך וה' יהיה עמך
Go, and G*d will be with you.

יברכך ה' וישמרך
G*d blesses you and watches over you.
יאר ה' פניו עליך ויחונך
G*d's grace is all around you.
ישא ה' פניו עליך וישם לך שלום
G*d wraps you in light and gives you peace.

G*d's angels are at your soul's side.
מימינה מיכאל
On her right, Mikha'el, carry our prayer;
משמאלה גבריאל
On her left, Gavriel, give her strength;
מאחורה רפאל
behind her, Rafa'el, heal all hurts;
לפניה אוריאל
before her, Uriel, light the way;
ומעל ראשה שכינת אל
all around her, *Shekhinat El*, G*d's Presence.

חזק ואמץ כי ה עמך
Be strong and of good courage; don't be afraid, for G*d is with you wherever you go.
פתחו לי שערי צדק אבוא בם אודה יה
Open the gates for me, that I may enter, and give thanks to G*d.
ה' ישמרך מכל רע ישמר את נפשך
G*d will keep you from all evil, will watch over your soul.
ה' ישמר צאתך ובואך מעתה ועד עולם
G*d will guard your leaving and your coming in eternally.

שמע ישראל ה' אלהינו ה' אחד
Shema Yisrael Adonai Eloheynu Adonai Ekhad

These lines are traditionally spoken to the departing soul at the end of the Jewish burial ritual; here they are used to reassure the soul and give her permission to leave the dying body.

*This is the Birkat Cohanim (Numbers 6.24-26), the ancient priestly blessing given by G*d to the High Priest, Aaron, to bless the Israelites.*

This blessing is recited as the final prayer of the bedtime Shema, *a collection of texts recited in a plea for safety through the coming night. As the dying person approaches the final night, this prayer invokes the hope of G*d's protection in death.*

An encouragement offered to the departing soul.

*The soul seeks to cross over the barriers that keep it from merging with G*d in life (Psalm 118.19).*

A final prayer for protection for the soul departing into the unknown (Psalm 121.7-8)

The departing soul recites the Shema, *or it is recited for her.*

Some Terms

Mitzvah (plural *mitzvot*) is a sacred obligation. According to Jewish tradition, nearly every human act undertaken mindfully can be understood as an opportunity for fulfilling such an obligation, and in so doing, each such act lifts up human life and makes it a work of art.

Midrash refers to an ancient form of interpretation applied to the Jewish sacred scriptures, especially Torah.

Torah consists of the first five books of the Jewish Bible. It is considered to be of a higher holiness than the rest of the Jewish scriptures (*Tanakh* in Hebrew), which consists of two sections called Prophets and Writings.

Tzedakah "justice" or "righteousness" is often used to refer to money given in honor of someone, living or dead.

Yizkor is a ritual marked by a special prayer recited by mourners for the dead. It is added to the regular prayers on the festivals of Pesakh (Passover), Shavuot, and Sukkot, and also on Yom Kippur.

Dying as a Jew

The Companion Volume to
The Alef-Bet of Death

G*d said to Avraham, "Come, and light the way before Me."
—*Bereshit Rabbah* 30:10

Contents

1. What It Means to Die as a Jew 55
2. Explaining *The Alef-Bet of Death* 58
3. A Note about G*d 60
4. More to Read—Background on the Jewish Themes
   Mentioned in *The Alef-Bet* 62

א *Alef*	Repentance	62
ב *Bet*	Contemplating the End...................................	63
ג *Gimmel*	Is It Permitted to Pray for Death?.................	64
ד *Dalet*	Avoidance, Panic, Bargaining, Anger, and Stubbornness: The Jewish Stages.................	69
ה *Hey*	Dying on Her Own Terms: The Death of Miriam	72
ו *Vahv*	Against Your Will	74
ז *Zayin*	*Z'va'ah*, the Jewish Ethical Wille	78
ח *Het*	The Body: Talmudic Teaching	80
ט *Tet*	The Dying Process	81
י *Yud*	Sharing a Loved One's Fear of Death: The Death of Aaron...	82
כ *Kaf*	A Jewish Interpretation of Death with Dignity Laws: Seven Teachings	84
ל *Lamed*	How to Die according to Jewish Ethical Teachings	87
מ *Mem*	*Tzedakah*—Provisions for the Journey........	94
נ *Nun*	Deathbed Teachings...	96
ס *Samekh*	"And Behold, Death Was Very Good"	97
ע *Ayin*	Bringing the Portrait of the King to the King	98
פ *Peh*	Death by a Kiss	102
צ *Tzadi*	The Soul: Jewish Mystical Teachings	103
ק *Kuf*	The Mourner's *Kaddish*	106
ר *Reysh*	Not Wanting to Die: The Death of Moses	107
ש *Shin*	Dying as a Jew	113
ת *Tahv*	G*d Is the *Mikveh* of Israel	114

Endnotes to Volume 2: Dying as a Jew.................................... 119

1. What It Means to Die as a Jew

> Existence embraces both life and death, and in a way death is the test of the meaning of life. If death is devoid of meaning, then life is absurd. Life's ultimate meaning remains obscure unless it is reflected upon in the face of death.[48]

The word used to describe the first Jew is *ivri*. The word as a verb means "crossing over." Abraham and Sarah symbolize the movement between what is and what will be, between the known here and now and the unknown over there. Jews are called many names by many peoples; even the name "Jew" was given by the Romans. But the Jewish way to describe ourselves is and has always been *Ivri*—the one who crosses over.

To cross over is to be in transition, not to be definitively either here or there; it is to find oneself only in movement. Dying is such a movement, and this transition is a sacred process.

The question of what will be at the end of this transition, whether or not there is some kind of life after death, is not addressed in the Hebrew sacred scriptures. The gift of life was enough for them, it seems; they did not ask for more than to be part of the sacred, eternal circle of life and death. Why expect more than to take one's turn, after life, as fertilizer for the next round of life? To be formed from earth, as our creation story describes, closes the circle perfectly, as we are returned to it.

In a different time, the rabbis of the Talmud do promulgate a doctrine of existence after the death of the body. It finds prominent expression in rabbinically created prayers in which G*d is called "the One who raises the dead to life."[49] It is possible that this belief derives its validity from Ezekiel's famous vision of the dry bones. If so, it mistakes the fate of the individual for that of the community. Ezekiel's vision was meant to encourage his fellow exiles to believe that the people of Israel were not wiped out; we would, someday, return to our land and live again as a people. We have much the same hope today, that we as a people will live on, even though you and I will die. Much of the measure of the meaning of our existence may be in that which we share with the people to which we belong in a future that we will never see but have helped to build.

Jewish tradition has never insisted on certainty regarding what is over there, beyond death. There is much entertaining speculation, and there are fascinating descriptions of a heaven in which the righteous sit with crowns on their heads and bask in the divine presence, or study Torah with G*d, or sit on a golden, three-legged stool, or even enjoy an abundant banquet.

We cannot know definitively what will be after we die. But we do know that as long as we live, our acts give meaning to life. The ethical choices you have made in your life will define you for others in this life after your death. You teach more than you know by the way that you live, and in Jewish tradition, it is a sacred obligation to tell stories about you after you are gone, so that your most shining moments may live on. Those of us who remember you will carry the impact of that memory with us, and in that way, a bit of you will live on within me. And in my turn, when I die, those around me will inherit from me the impact of my life upon them—and something of you will be part of that.

The manner of one's death cannot nullify life's meaning. Some die suddenly, some die in terrible ways, some have their lives taken from them by evil or misfortune—but no life is defined by the manner of death.

It is all gathered into one gift: the quality of one's life and of one's death becomes one whole story, and each gives meaning to the other. As Rabbi Nakhman of Bratslav taught, every day of our lives, we work on the portrait of the image of G*d that each of us is.[50] Each day, we add to the portrait, change a line here or add one there, choose a color, or erase a whole swath and start over. Not until the last day will the portrait be complete, and it will be given to those who remember you to behold it and to understand, finally, the meaning of your life.

Death, when one is gifted with time to face it, offers a chance to refine the meaning of one's life. Approaching death is not a time of stasis but of opportunity. There is much to learn, to understand, and to teach.

What this book seeks to offer you is a path toward helping your mind and your spirit find peace in what your body already knows. Brief teachings from Jewish tradition are offered to help you think about your situation and your choices.

There are Jewish traditions that will show you that you need not die feeling that you are an isolated, lonely individual. As a Jew, you are part of a community that embraces you with ancient ritual and with ready community—no matter how long you have been gone from it and no matter how far you have felt distanced.

You will continue to teach those around you until your last moments, and possibly even after, in ways that you cannot fully comprehend or control, but simply by continuing to be who you are and by doing what you will decide to do as you follow this path from life to death.

2. Explaining *The Alef-Bet of Death*

A guide to dying is not a new idea. The *Ars Moriendi,* a Christian guide to dying, was written in the fifteenth century in the aftermath of the Black Death. There are examples of such guides in other religious traditions as well.

The Jewish guide to dying is arranged by way of the Hebrew *alef-bet* and its twenty-two letters. The companion volume offers more to read should you wish to explore the concepts presented briefly in *The Alef-Bet of Death.* The letters and the teachings they convey invite you to explore the meaning you may find in your death. You may find support for the path you walk in the teachings and stories it conveys.

According to Jewish mystical lore, the universe and everything in it was created by way of the twenty-two letters of the Hebrew *alef-bet.* Modern science tells us that all of physical life is based on molecules—our DNA—known by only four letters: *A, C, G,* and *T.* This suggests that the physical aspect of our existence really is simple, and it hints at how quickly we might move beyond it, to the deeper and more complex levels that give our physical existence its meaning.

When those four letters, representing the physical level of our lives, are subtracted from the twenty-two of the Hebrew *alef-bet*, we are left with eighteen, the numerical value of the Hebrew word *hai*, "life." With insights from all twenty-two Hebrew letters, we will explore the emotional, intellectual, and spiritual levels of life that define the hai of your life.

Here is an example of how the letter *bet* can teach us. It is the first letter of the first verse of the Torah:

> *B'Reyshit,* "[with] First," *bara Elohim* "G*d created" *et hashamayim* "the heavens" *v'et ha-aretz* "and the earth." (Genesis 1:1)

Strangely, the first word of the Torah is a grammatical impossibility. The letter *bet* is affixed, as a prefix meaning "with" or "in," to the word "first," constructed as if at the beginning of a list: first, you take a cup of flour; second, you add an egg; third ... The word *b'reyshit* is only clumsily translated "in the beginning," and that *bet,* hanging there awkwardly, drew attention to itself in the eyes of the commentators and interpreters. Why would the world begin with the letter *bet,* anyway?

> Rabbi Yonah said in the name of Rabbi Levi, "the world was created with a ב - a letter which is closed on all sides, and open only in front. This is to indicate that you are not permitted to inquire of what is below, what is above, and what is behind you, but only from the moment of the creation and onward."[51]

Our understanding is limited and does not permit us to discover all that we want and need to know. Life and death will remain, on some level, as mysterious as a wide river's dark and mysterious depths. But those waters are not alien to you; you are a part of them, and they of you. And all, you and the depths and the fear, are within G*d.

3. A Note about G*d

There are many ways to approach G*d or the idea of G*d.

In Jewish tradition, it is possible to conceive of G*d as a compassionate, personal, intimate support for you. Even if you hide behind a pillar and whisper, it is said, G*d hears your prayer.

It is also possible to think of G*d as an abundant, overflowing well, the Source of all life from which we draw the energy of our being.

It is also possible to be very angry at G*d, as Job questions G*d in his time of death and despair. There is a mystery at the heart of life that we will never understand, and it is also true that the mystery of G*d is one that is entirely beyond us. This is the stark, terrifying abyss of darkness and incomprehension that is also human experience.

G*d might be understood as the eternity, all space and time, in which we exist in a particular place, for one brief moment. Not at all a personality—more like a medium. As a Jewish mystic suggested, if we were fish, G*d would be the sea. If G*d is eternity, you are that which participates in a moment of time in that eternity.

The prophet Jeremiah called G*d the *Mikveh*, the Hope, of Israel. The great sage Rabbi Akiva, many generations later, explicated: even as Jews traditionally immerse in the waters of a *mikveh* in order to effect a transition from one personal state of being to another, so might we undergo a transformational experience when we immerse ourselves in hope.

You do not have to give up hope in order to accept death. There is always hope for the healing power of wholeness, acceptance, and peace, even when there cannot be healing of the body. There is such a thing as a good death, and perhaps for you, a step toward it can be found within these pages.

Jews are the people who fall in and out of belief about G*d every day—but never about the beauty and meaning of the path from life to death. You do not have to believe in G*d in order to draw wisdom as water from this guide to dying. You only have to be willing to immerse yourself in the hope that you too are surrounded by a presence—the presence of G*d in Jewish tradition as it is reflected here.

As it has been said, "You can never fall out of the hands of G*d."

Because we can never truly know G*d or name that which is beyond us, this book follows the Jewish tradition of not spelling the name out completely. Let the asterisk between the first and last letters offer you two thoughts: First, the asterisk is often used to indicate a footnote—further levels of exploration of an idea; in the same way, this asterisk does point to many more levels of thought. Second, let the asterisk reassure you: there is a mystery here that is beyond human reason and imagination and will never be understood in life, but Jewish tradition teaches us that each one of us in turn will encounter that mystery and see something illuminated in those moments, something that you could never see in life, in your dying.

4. More to Read—Background on the Jewish Themes Mentioned in *The Alef-Bet*

א *Alef*
Repentance

The story is told of an unlikely midrashic hero named El'azar ben Dordai, a sex addict who visits prostitutes regularly until one of them declares to him that his *teshuvah*, repentance, will never be accepted. In his panic, El'azar searches for someone to intercede for him, just as we look for extenuating circumstances to plead for us. But all of creation is in need of mercy, everyone has regrets, and no one can answer for another's life. Finally, he realizes this:

> Said he: The matter then depends upon me alone! Having placed his head between his knees, he wept aloud until his soul departed. Then a *bat kol* was heard proclaiming: "Rabbi El'azar ben Dordai is destined for the life of the world to come!" ... [Upon hearing the story] Rabbi Judah haNasi wept and said: One may acquire eternal life after many years, another in one hour! Rabbi also said: Those who return are not just accepted, they are even called "Rabbi"![52]

A *bat kol* (often translated "heavenly voice" but may also be usefully understood as the still, small voice of conscience) is heard proclaiming that El'azar's *teshuvah* is accepted. It is accepted because it is clearly genuine. The eternal life that El'azar achieves at the moment of his death is the rehabilitation of his name and reputation; he is even called rabbi, an honorable title indicating one who has something important to teach. In a final, gentle moment of humor, the midrash also pokes a bit of fun at the chagrined head rabbi of the community, Judah haNasi. No doubt Rabbi

Judah has been urging El'azar to turn away from his behavior for years, as he should have, but that does not invalidate the integrity of his turning when he does.

There are two turnings, and although they are intertwined, they stand separately. Wronging another requires facing that other and making amends; the "victimless crime" that no other witnesses belongs to another category, that of "between a person and G*d." All the sincere prayers in the world will not move the former.

> R. Elazar b. Azariah taught this interpretation: From all your sins you shall be made pure before HaShem (Leviticus 16:30) "for transgressions between a person and the Ever Present One does the Day of Atonement atone, but for transgressions between a person and one's fellow, the Day of Atonement atones only if the person regains the other's goodwill."[53]

Of course, there may be those who will not accept an apology and who refuse to let go of the stubborn anger in which they have taken refuge. Jewish law provides an answer. When you have asked sincerely for forgiveness, specifying the offense and demonstrating true turning, true *teshuvah*, from the former path that gave offense, then if the offended person withholds forgiveness, the guilt of that offense is no longer yours but theirs.

ב *Bet*
Contemplating the End

The Jewish mystics imagine the inner earthquake of the day of death:

> The dying one's horizon is suddenly widened, just before the eyes close forever, like a flame that spurts up just before it is extinguished, and one is permitted to see what could not be seen during life. "We have learned: when one lies on one's deathbed and judgment rests upon one decreeing that one will leave this world, one is granted

an additional supernal spirit that one never had before. And when this dwells within, one sees what one has never seen before ... and once this has been granted, and one sees, one departs from this world. This is the meaning of "You add their spirit; they perish and return to their dust" (Psalm 104:29) and "no one can see Me and live" (Exodus 33:20)—in one's lifetime one cannot; in death one can.[54]

What is a Jew to do in the face of such longing and such terror? The traditional Jewish answer: recite Psalms.

Psalm 23

If G*d is with me I will lack for nothing.
I will walk in tranquil meadows,
alongside serene waters;
my soul will be at rest.
Even when I walk in the valley of the shadow of death,
I will be at peace,
knowing that I am part of the circle of life and death
embracing all the world.
The table is set for me, my cup overflows;
O that goodness and mercy reach out for me,
and let me know that I dwell in the House of G*d always.

ג *Gimmel*
Is It Permitted to Pray for Death?

In the Babylonian Talmud (Ketubot 104a) we find recorded:

> On the day when Rebbe died, the Rabbis decreed a public fast (because of his illness) and offered prayers for heavenly mercy. They announced that whoever said that Rebbe has died should be stabbed with a sword.

> The maidservant of Rebbe ascended the roof and said: "The angels desire Rebbe to join them and the mortals

desire Rebbe to remain with them. May it be the will of G*d that the mortals may overpower the angels." When, however, she saw how often he entered the latrine (on account of his stomach sickness), painfully taking off his *tefillin* and putting them on again, she prayed: "May it be the will of G*d that the angels may overpower the mortals." As the Rabbis did not cease their prayers for heavenly mercy, she took up a small earthenware jar and threw it down from the roof to the ground. For a brief moment (as they heard the sound of the breaking jar), they ceased praying and Rebbe died.

Jewish law, *halakhah,* is a carefully defined process of discerning G*d's will in the world and instructing the Jew how to follow it in specific cases. Over millennia, the *mitzvot*, "commandments" of the Torah, have been applied according to a balance between the meaning and spirit of the law itself and its meeting with the details of each new situation. The generations of legal discussions that guided Jewish life for two thousand years are recorded in the Talmud, and later, specific case law can be found in the multitudes of books that come after it. The *Shulkhan Arukh* is the best known of these.

In all of the legal writings of Judaism, rulings are formulated correctly only when existing law is balanced with specific circumstances. This process is developed through Jewish legal discussions and rulings expressed in the form of *she'elot uteshuvot,* literally "questions and answers." Referred to in English as *responsa,* the genre consists of rabbinic "answers," each addressing a specific legal question. In short, there is no one correct answer for any question, because all depends upon the judgment between broad legal and ethical concepts and striking the correct balance between past and present, as well as between judgment and mercy.

Jewish law insists upon the sanctity of life and its preservation; *pikuah nefesh,* the "saving of a life," supersedes all other *mitzvot*. This statement of the overarching concept is not the last word, however. The specifics of an individual case must be considered; among them, how does one define "life"? And when is medical action no longer "saving"?

In 1840, the question of whether a patient should be kept alive, preventing death at all costs, came before the chief rabbi of the Jewish community of Smyrna (today's Izmir, on the western coast of Turkey). Rabbi Hayim Palaggi (1788–1869) was highly respected as a *halakhic* (legal) authority and wrote many responsa on various subjects of concern to the Jews of his time. The question and the answer both express the belief of the time that prayer and the giving of *tzedakah* were as efficacious as we consider modern medicine to be today.[55]

Question:

> A G*d-fearing scholar has a pious wife. For our many sins, the woman has been sick with a long, enduring illness for more than twenty years. She is plagued and crushed with pain. Her hands and legs are shriveled up and she is therefore housebound. This woman has borne these sufferings patiently and her husband has met them without bitterness. He has not troubled her even for an instant. On the contrary, he shows her special love, so that she should not fear that he may be resenting the burden.
>
> This woman, because of her great pain, prays to G*d that He take her life so that she may find rest from suffering. Her sons bring her physicians and many medicines and have hired a servant for her that she should have no household worries. But her pains have now greatly increased and even the doctors have despaired of her recovery from this sickness. She pleads with her husband and her sons that they should pray for her death and asks particularly that her sons ask G*d's mercy for her to take her life. But her husband and her sons do not listen to her. On the contrary, they seek out scholars to study on her behalf. They continue to give *tzedakah* and atonements and oil for the candelabra of the synagogue, in order to obtain healing for her.

> Now teach us, O righteous teacher, whether there is any prohibition involved if they should really pray for her to die in order that she may find rest ...

Answer:

The first part of the answer consists of a general discussion of obligation described in the Talmud, by which a husband is bound to love and cherish and protect his wife; of how wrong it is, according to the Talmudic law, even to think of her death, if, for example, he wishes she were dead, that he might marry someone else.

> But all this [the prohibition against wishing one's wife dead] applies only when such wishes are without her knowledge or due to hatred. But here, where she wishes it herself and can no longer endure her pain, under these circumstances it is possible to say that it is permitted (to wish, or even to pray for her death). I come to this conclusion from what the Talmud says in *Ketubot* 104a. We are there told that on the day on which Rabbi Judah haNasi was to die, the rabbis decreed a fast and said that anyone who should say that Rabbi has died would be put to death. The servant-maid of Rabbi Judah went up to the roof and she said, "the angels seek Rabbi Judah; the earthlings seek him too; may the earthlings conquer the angels." But when she saw how much suffering Rabbi Judah underwent, she changed and said, "may the angels conquer the earthlings." But the rabbis continued to pray for his recovery. She then threw a pitcher from the roof among them. This interrupted their prayer. And he died.
>
> Now it is made clear in this section of the Talmud that the servant-maid of Rabbi Judah saw his great pain. Furthermore, we know from the Talmud and the later scholars that they learned laws from this servant-woman (she was a learned woman). She was full of wisdom and

> piety. Therefore we may learn from her this law, that it is permitted to ask mercy for a very sick person that he may die, so that his soul may come to rest. For if this action of hers were not according to the law, the Talmud would not have quoted it; or, if they had quoted it, simply because it was an incident that occurred, and they did not think that she had done well (in stopping the rabbis in their prayers) the Talmud would have said so. As for the rabbis who continued to pray that he should live, they did not know Rabbi Judah's suffering as much as the servant-maid did …
>
> So the law emerges in our case that this woman who suffers all these agonies, and asks that others prayer for her that she die, it is certainly completely permitted them to do so. I have also seen the words of Rabbenu Nissim to *Nedarim* 44a, in which he says, "It seems to me that there are times when it is necessary to pray for the sick that he die; as, for example, if the sick person suffers greatly and it is (in any case) impossible for him to continue living much longer."

Palaggi continues with the caution that there is some danger that people might think ill of the sons for praying that she die, although they have every right to. People may imagine that they are trying to get rid of the burden. Yet, on the other hand, they cannot pray that she should live and continue to suffer. He concludes with the following counsel.

> But others, who are not related and would be free of any of these suspicions, if they would pray that she should die and find rest, they may do so; for it is all for a high purpose and G*d searches the heart.
>
> As it is said in *The Book of the Pious,* no. 234, that we must not cry out aloud at the time when the soul is departing, in order not to cause the soul to return (i.e. not to revive

> the dying person's hold on life) and bear more pain. Why did Kohelet say "There is a time to die"? It means that, when the time comes for a soul to go forth, people should not cry aloud so that it returns, for the person can only live a very short time and in that short time must bear great pain. That is why it is written, "There is a time to live and a time to die."
>
> Here you have it explicitly from the words of *The Book of the Pious*, that there is no justification for praying for one who is already dying. See also what Isserles says in *Yoreh De'ah* 339. This is what, to my humble opinion, I have written hastily, for my strength is weak and may the Almighty G*d say "Enough" to our troubles, deliver us from error, and show us wonders from His Law. Amen.

Other Jewish authorities have offered commentaries upon the question of whether it is permitted to pray for the death of one who is in great agony and cannot be cured. As the twentieth-century Jewish scholar Dr. Louis Jacobs noted in 1967, much of the Jewish law forbidding such prayer argues against such without a clearly demonstrated basis.

> Surely in matters of this nature, personal feelings cannot so easily be set aside. We do tend to speak of a 'merciful release'. How can a person who sincerely feels this to be so be prevented from pouring out his heart to G*d? It is surely no accident that ... none of the earlier authorities lay down the law on this matter ... it is only the much later authorities who apply the halakhah to this case, and it may seriously be questioned whether to do this is an advantage.[56]

ד *Dalet*
Avoidance, Panic, Bargaining, Anger, and Stubbornness: The Jewish Stages

On Yom Kippur afternoon, Jews gathered in congregations everywhere in the world hear recited the story of the prophet Jonah. This short book of four chapters is understood by ancient Jewish commentary to be an exploration of the repentance to which we are all called on that holy day. Even as repentance—an honest reckoning with one's life—is the essence of a good and conscious death, the story of Jonah can be read as a metaphor for the process of accepting one's own mortality.

Chapter 1. Jonah, a prophet, is called by G*d to go to Nineveh, "that great city,"[57] to proclaim within it the downfall that is coming, because of the sinful behavior of the inhabitants. Jonah's immediate reaction is *avoidance*. Rather than heading east toward his duty, he goes down to the Jaffa port and books passage on the next ship anywhere. This happens to be going to Tarshish, a place that in ancient Israel was considered to be at the ends of the earth, far from knowledge of G*d.

It is not unusual for us when we are avoiding an important truth to believe that we are capable of doing so without inconveniencing our companions on the journey, but it is usually not so. And so it is with Jonah. The ship experiences a deadly storm, and all are required to help bail—or, in the parallel activity of the time, to pray—but Jonah remains below decks, fast asleep, entirely unaware of the peril his behavior is causing.

Avoidance ends when Jonah see that he has placed the entire ship and all those upon it in peril of their lives, and he realizes his responsibility. "Heave me overboard, and the sea will calm down for you; for I know that this terrible storm came upon you on my account." They are loathe to abandon Jonah to the fate he has created for himself, but when they do, the sea around them calms immediately.

Chapter 2. Jonah is overwhelmed and terrified by the abyss into which he feels swallowed. In his *panic*, he cries out for help, in a beautiful stylized text similar to that of the Psalms:

> Out of the belly of the grave I cried,
> and You heard my voice.
> For You cast me into the depth,

> In the heart of the seas, And the flood was around me;
> All Your waves and Your billows Passed over me.
> And I said: 'I have been cast out From before Your eyes';
> Yet I will look again Toward Your holy temple.
> The waters circled me about, even to the soul;
> The deep was around me; The weeds were wrapped around my head.
> I went down to the bottoms of the mountains;
> The earth with her bars closed over me forever.

In his extremis, Jonah makes promises, *bargaining* for his life:

> When my soul fainted within me, I remembered HaShem;
> And my prayer came in to You, Into Your holy Temple.
> Those who respect lying vanities abandon mercy.
> But I will sacrifice to You with the voice of thanksgiving;
> What I have vowed I will pay. Only G*d can save!

Chapter 3. Back on dry land, Jonah makes his way to Nineveh. He does what he is told: walking around the great city, he proclaims over and over again, "Forty days more, and Nineveh shall be overthrown!" And a surprising thing occurs: the people of Nineveh believe Jonah, and they all, from the king to the commoner, give themselves over to repentance. When G*d saw their sincerity, "G*d renounced the punishment that had been planned for them, and did not carry it out."

Chapter 4. Jonah is *angry* at this turn of events. "Isn't this just what I said when I was still in my own country?" Despite the fact that the narrative describes no such discussion with the divine, Jonah remembers that he did, and now he has been proved correct. All his journey was a waste, and now he will be considered a liar.

"I know that you are a compassionate and gracious G*d, slow to anger, abounding in kindness, renouncing punishment. Please, G*d, take my life, for I would rather die than live!" And G*d responded, "Are you that greatly angry?"

Jonah stalks out of the city and finds a place at a distance to watch and see whether anything will happen in Nineveh. He waits, *stubbornly* holding on to his anger. G*d causes a castor bean plant with large leaves to grow over Jonah to shade him; "Jonah was very happy about the plant." But then G*d caused a worm to attack the plant, and it withered, and then a hot east wind began to blow. Jonah, still angry, once again prayed to G*d to kill him: "I would rather die than live."

Then G*d said to Jonah, "Are you so deeply angry about the plant?"

"Yes," he replied, "so deeply that I want to die."

Then G*d said, "You cared about the plant, which you did not work for and which you did not grow, which appeared overnight and perished overnight. And should I not care about Nineveh, that great city, in which there are more than a hundred and twenty thousand persons who do not yet know their right hand from their left, and also much cattle!"

This is the end of the book. We don't know how Jonah responds, or whether he attains any understanding, at the end of this story of his. Similarly, the end of the journey of life does not necessarily bring closure or understanding, although we hope that each of us will know that blessing.

ה *Hey*
Dying on Her Own Terms: The Death of Miriam

This teaching[58] is an excerpt from *Eysh Kodesh (Holy Fire)*, the writings of Rabbi Kalonymus Shapira. Rabbi Shapira was a rabbi of the Warsaw Ghetto; there he lost, one by one, his son, his daughter, his wife, and many friends and companions. The text below is from his teaching on the part of the Torah named Hukkat in 1942, which was his wife's *yahrzeit*, the anniversary of her death. By poignant coincidence, her name was Miriam. This surprisingly radical teaching was imparted shortly before the liquidation of the ghetto, which led to the final, doomed revolt. Rabbi Shapira did not survive.

[It is written in the Book] *BaMidbar*[59] "And Miriam died there"[60] (Numbers 20:1) "… and the community had no water" (Numbers 20:2), for the well was there by the merit of Miriam … We will examine what this might hint to us.

Rashi [medieval Bible commentator Rabbi Shlomo Yitzhaki] writes that Miriam also died by a kiss [from G*d]; and if so, why is this not said [in Torah] about her, that she died by a kiss from the mouth of G*d? [Answers Rashi:] because this is not the way of showing honor in heaven.[61] And what is hinted to us from this? Why should there be any sense that this is a case in which G*d is showing, or not showing, respect? After all, it is not as if—perish the thought—it was an actual physical kiss!

We can understand this from my father's teachings, he who was Rabbi before me (may the memory of the righteous holy ones be for a blessing). He taught that the Jew must understand that, when there is a feeling of rising up from below, this is really only because the Holy One has caused the sense of knowledge and desire from above, so that there should be a feeling of rising up from below. There is support for this in other holy books, such as in the verse from Psalms, "you are a merciful G*d, for you reward us according to our acts" (Psalm 62:13). In truth, it is G*d who stirs the individual, and gives the strength and the desire, as we said above, to act to do the right thing. If not, no reward would ever come to the individual, for in truth, G*d who is the One Who Acts. This is the mercy G*d shows! G*d rewards the individual as if it were the individual who initiated the action: "you are a merciful G*d, for your reward us according to our act."—thus far [my father's] holy words.

So we see that according to this, when a woman becomes a Righteous One, studying Torah and fulfilling *mitzvot*, this is really of her own doing, for she is not obligated to the *mitzvot*. Nevertheless, she acts—and not because she was roused from above. This is the meaning of our assertion that [Miriam] also died by a kiss from the mouth of G*d. Why, then, is it not mentioned that she died by a kiss from the mouth of G*d, that this is not the way of respect in heaven? Only this: she had achieved a level of insight so great as this, which was not caused by G*d, but by her own rising from below.

Therefore it is not written "from the mouth of G*d", for the source of her effort was within her, and flowed forth from her.

Therefore the well, the flowing source of living waters, holy waters, existed because of her merit.

ו *Vahv*
Against Your Will

The following is a long mythical midrash in which the rabbis of the Talmudic era tell speculative stories about the fate of the soul. It is not a statement of required belief; Judaism maintains within its many teachings a great diversity of beliefs regarding the soul and whether there is any existence for it apart from the body.

> While the fetus is still in the womb, it is taught the entire Torah. As it emerges into the air of this world, an angel comes and slaps it on the mouth, making it forget all the Torah it had learned. It does not leave the womb until it is made to take an oath. And what is this oath?
>
> "Be righteous and do not be wicked.
>
> And even if the whole world calls you righteous, do not consider yourself to be what they say.

Know that the Holy Blessed One, is pure, and his servants are pure, and the soul which he has given to you is pure. If you preserve its purity—fine. If not, it will be taken away from you."

Then the Holy Blessed One summons the angel who is in charge of souls and says, "Bring me So-and-So's soul." The soul immediately comes before the Holy Blessed One, and bows before Him.

The Holy Blessed One says to it, "Enter this drop." The soul then says, "Master of the World, since I was created, this world has been good to me. If it is all right with you, please do not put me into this stinking drop, because I am holy and pure."

The Holy Blessed One says to the soul, "the world which you will enter is better than this world, and, besides, when I created you, I only created you for this drop."

The Holy Blessed One then forces the soul into the drop, and the angel returns the drop, with the soul, into the mother's womb. He also stations two angels there to prevent miscarriages.

Candle sits on its head, and by its light the developing fetus sees from one end of the world to the other.

In the morning, the angel takes it on a tour of the Garden of Eden, showing it the Righteous sitting in great majesty.

The angel says, "do you know whose soul that one is?"

"No," he replies.

The angel says, the one you see treated there with such honor and majesty was created just like you in the mother's womb. And this one, and that one, too. And they kept G*d's way carefully. If you do as they did, then, after your death, as after theirs, you will be privileged to enjoy all this grandeur and this honor—just as you see it now. But if you do not act that way, you will find yourself in another place … which I will show you.

In the evening, he takes it to Gehinnom and shows it wicked people being beaten with fiery clubs by angels of destruction. They are screaming, *"oy v'avoi!!"* No mercy is shown to them.

The angel says, "My child, do you know who these people are who are being burned?"

And he answers, "No, I do not."

The angel responds, "Know that these, too, were created from a stinking drop in the mother's womb. They entered the world, but did not keep the ways of the Holy Blessed One. That is why they have been reduced to such degradation."

The angel takes him around to every place where he will ever be, and to his future home, and to where he will be buried, and then takes him back to the womb.

Then the Holy Blessed One sets up double doors and a crossbar to the womb and says, "For now, you may go only this far—no farther."

When it is time for the fetus to be born, the same angel comes and says, "Go! Your time to be born has arrived."

But the fetus says, "But have I not already told the Holy Blessed One, I am satisfied in the world where I am?"

The Angel replies, "The world I am taking you into is beautiful. Furthermore, whether you wanted it or not, you were created, and, against your will, you will be born."

At the moment of birth, the infant weeps.

Why does he weep?

He weeps for that world is leaving.

And he weeps because, at that moment, they show him seven worlds: in the first world, he is like a king—everyone looks after him in runs to see him, and hugs and kisses him ... until he is a year old.

In the second world, he is like a pig—always in the garbage, and a mess to clean ... until he is two.

In the third world, he is like a baby goat dancing in the meadow—always dancing everywhere ... until he is five.

In the fourth world, he is like a horse, proudly prancing down the road—this is what a child is like, full of pride and sure of the powers of youth ... until he is eighteen.

In the fifth world, he is like a mule with a saddle on his back—with the wife and sons and daughters, running around looking for a livelihood to support the members of his household.

In the sixth world, he is like a dog, still grabbing for a livelihood wherever he can, sometimes being pushy, taking and stealing from one and then others without shame.

In the seventh world, he does not resemble anything, having become different from all other things—even his family curses him and wishes he were dead, and even infants make fun of him.

Finally, when his time comes to die, the angel comes to him and says, "Do you recognize me?"

And he answers, "Yes. But why have you come to me today?"

The angel answers, "To take you away from this world."

He weeps deeply—a weeping that can be heard around the world, though no human being can hear it—and he says to the angel, "Have you not already taken me from two worlds and put me in this one?"

And the angel replies, "but have I not already told you, 'against your will you were created, and were born, and will die, and will—against your will—give an accounting to the King of Kings of Kings, the Holy Blessed One'?"[62]

ז *Zayin*
Z'va'ah, the Jewish Ethical Will

Why does the mind so often choose to fly away at the moment the word waited for all one's life is about to be spoken?[63]

What did you mean by the way you lived your life? What are the values by which you tried to live? And why is it often so difficult to express what is most important?

Within Jewish tradition, there is a rich vein of writing called the *z'va'ah*, translated as "ethical will." Even as we prepare a will to ensure that the material assets that we leave behind will be used in a way we would intend, in premodern Jewish tradition, it was considered praiseworthy for a person to write another kind of will, in an effort to leave behind not only material but spiritual assets.

The *z'va'ah*, ethical will, is a letter, written or dictated by you, or a voice recording if writing is not possible. It is a message from you to those you leave behind. It gives you the chance to explain what you meant by the way you lived your life.

The patriarch Jacob's recitation upon his deathbed is often cited as the first example of an ethical will. A more complete document is that of the medieval Gluckl of Hameln. This long letter to her children described her life's events, her choices, and her struggles, always with a sense of her own understanding of why she acted as she did. The document is full of the quotes, from Jewish tradition and elsewhere, that informed her sense of her acts and molded what became herself.

Many less well-known ethical wills have been entrusted to eternity by those who knew they were going to die; many were shorter, some dashed off in a hurry before the journey from which there would be no return. Some were written at leisure; others consist of only a few words, scrawled on the inside of a boxcar headed to Treblinka.

Especially with those to whom we are closest, so much goes unspoken, and we are so often unable to express all that is in our hearts. Those who offer the hesped, the words spoken about you at the funeral, will do their best to describe and interpret the meaning of your life, the "portrait of the King" that you have brought to the King.[64] You may feel that your life's acts should speak for themselves, and no doubt to an extent they do. Yet there are those who love you who long for you to open your heart to them as only you can. And there are those who, because of physical or emotional distance, cannot hear you now and cannot see your acts for what you meant by them.

In the writing of a *z'va'ah*, you confront the imperfect nature of human mortality, your own as well as ours. What you meant is not necessarily what came across. You do have this chance to set it down for others and, in so doing, think it over yourself. In this way, you may become more aware of what you actually cared about in your life. What did you mean by the way you lived? What values did you try to live by? And what words do you want to be remembered by?

ח *Het*
The Body: Talmudic Teaching

The Holy One's creatures borrow from each other and repay each other. It is only mortals who borrow from each other and then seek to swallow each other with usurious interest and cheating.

> He who exacts interest says to the Holy One, "why do You not take payment from Your world in which Your creatures are – from the earth, to which you give drink; from the flowers, which You make grow; from the lights, which You cause to shine; from the soul, which You breathe into the body, from the body, which You preserve?"
>
> The Holy One replies, "see how much I lend, yet take no interest, and how much the earth lends and takes no interest. I take only the capital I lent, even as the earth takes her capital, as Scripture declares: *The dust returns to the earth as it was, and the spirit returns to G*d who gave it.*"[65]
>
> At one time, providing decent burial was more burdensome for relatives of the dead than the death itself, so they would leave the body and run away. Then the wealthy Rabban Gamaliel II prescribed a simple style for himself; he was carried out in inexpensive linen shrouds. Thereafter, everyone followed his example, and carried out their dead in inexpensive linen shrouds. Rav Papa added: And now, it is the practice to take out the dead even in a shroud of rough cloth worth no more than a *zuz*. (Mo'ed Katan 27b)

A *zuz* is the equivalent of four *perutot,* which was the smallest coin in use in Second Temple period Israel. In today's valuation, it has been estimated at anywhere from $7.50 to $20.00. "Whoever heaps elaborate shrouds upon the dead transgresses the prohibition *bal tashkhit,* 'do not waste,' against wanton destruction, according to Rabbi Meir."[66]

One should not assume that burial rituals were simple just because the casket and shrouds are inexpensive. For example, it is mandated that "even the poorest man in Israel should provide [for his wife's funeral] not less than two flutes and at least one professional female mourner."[67]

Taharah: "cleansing," preparation of the body for burial by the *Hevra Kadisha.*

Taharah has five stages:

Mekhilah—introductory prayers, including one asking forgiveness from the deceased, and others readying the members of the *hevra kaddisha* for their sacred work.
Rekhitzah—physical washing of the body.
Taharah—ritual washing of the body.
Halbashah—dressing the body.
Halanah—placing the body in the *aron* (casket), along with concluding prayers.

ט *Tet*
The Dying Process

Dying is much like being born, and a dying person may experience three distinct phases of dying: prelabor, active labor, and death. The labor of dying is often marked by specific emotional and physical changes:

Physical State	**Emotional/Spiritual State**

*Preactive Labor*_____

- increase in pain, confusion, and weakness
- withdrawal, frequent crying
- varied sleep and wake patterns
- fear of being alone

- heightened sensitivity to sight, sound, smell, and activity
- restlessness, agitation, anxiety, fear
- anger and impatience with loved ones
- need to discuss death

Active Labor

- irregular breathing
- needing permission to let go of life
- skin cooling
- calmness, acceptance
- deterioration in awareness
- a sense of being out of body
- inability to respond verbally
- a sense of a spiritual source[68]

Death

׳ *Yud*
Sharing a Loved One's Fear of Death: The Death of Aaron

> G*d said to Moses, "Do Me a favor and tell Aaron about his death, for I am ashamed to tell him." Said R. Huna in the name of R. Tanhum bar Hiyya: What did Moses do? He rose early in the morning and went over to Aaron's place.
>
> He began calling out, "Aaron, my brother!"
>
> Aaron came down to him and asked, "How is it that you have come here so early today?"
>
> Moses answered, "There is a thing, a problem from the Torah that I was mulling over during the night, and it gave me great difficulty. That is why I have come over to visit you so early in the morning."

Aaron asked, "What is the problem?"

Moses answered, "I don't know what it was—but I do know that it is in the book of Genesis. Bring it, and let us read in it." They took the book of Genesis and read in it, story by story, and at each one Aaron said, "G*d did well, G*d created well." But when they came to the creation of Adam, Moses said, "What shall I say about Adam who brought death to the world?" Aaron replied, "My brother Moses, you surely would not say that in this we do not accept the decree of G*d? …

Then Moses said, "What about me—who had control over the ministering angels? And what about you—who halted the spread of death? Is our end not the same? We have another few years to live—perhaps twenty years?" Aaron said, "That is only a few years." Moses brought the number down more and more, and spoke of the very day of death.

Immediately, Aaron's bones felt as if they were quaking. He said, "Perhaps the thing was for me?"

Moses answered, "yes."

Immediately, the Israelites saw that his stature had shrunk, as it is said, "The whole community saw that Aaron was about to die [literally, had died]." (Numbers 20:29)

Then Aaron said, "My heart is dead within me, and the terror of death has fallen upon me."

Moses asked him, "Do you accept death?"

And he answered, "Yes."[69]

כ *Kaf*
A Jewish Interpretation of Death with Dignity Laws: Seven Teachings

Jewish legal and wisdom literature speaks not of rights but of human responsibilities and privileges that flow from our sense that life is a gift to be honored. Two verses set up our dialectic: the command to "choose life" in Deuteronomy 30:19 and the observation of Ecclesiastes 3:2, "There is a time to be born, and a time to die."

1. One of the great purposes of religion is that of helping us to face our own human finitude. We all face death. We are commanded to pass through death as we have passed through life, doing the best we can to uphold the ethical values that give meaning to our lives. Humility is our human value here, not arrogance. With all our technology, we are not more powerful than death.

> When a patient is, as it were, actually in the clutches of the angel of death and the death process has actually begun, there is no obligation to heal.[70]

2. Jewish religious values celebrate life but not as an end in itself. Religious writings make it clear that life is meant to be lived as an expression of one's values and sense of meaning. Life is not an absolute value but a value relative to its meaning.

> If you are threatened with the choice of violation of Torah or death, you should commit the transgression rather than be killed, as it is written "you shall live by them" (Leviticus 18:5)—live by them, not die by them ... whoever abstains from a transgression, or performs a good deed for no selfish reason, such as fear, or vanity ... sanctifies the Name of G*d.[71]

3. By teaching that we are all equally created as reflections of the image of G*d, Jewish religious values teach respect for each individual, including respect for choices made by others with which we do not agree but which are thoughtfully reached.

> An old woman came before Rabbi Yose ben Halafta and said to him: "Master, I have grown so very old that my life has become hideous. I find no taste in food or drink, and I wish to depart from the world." He asked, "how did you extend your life so long?" She replied, "Whenever I have something to do, however enjoyable it may be, I am in the habit of putting it aside early every morning and going to the synagogue. He said, "for three days, one after another, keep yourself away from the synagogue." She went off and did as he advised, and on the third day she took sick and died.[72]

4. Jewish religious values recognize that we individuals interact in community and teach us that we must take great care with each other and that the world itself depends upon it: *al shlosha d'varim ha'olam omeyd: al haTorah, al haAvodah, v'al gemilut hasadim*, "on three things the world depends: on learning, on prayer, and on kindness" (Pirke Avot 1:2).

5. Regarding the concern that a successfully applied law could yet be cause for abuse or disrespect of human life: Jewish religious values call it sin when we fail to act for others, hiding behind the fear that something bad might happen; we are called upon not to inflict our fears upon others but to show courage in our lives and in our own and each other's deaths.

> That which is hateful to you, do not do to another person.[73]

6. Jewish religious values teach that our responsibility to each other is to help each other achieve a life of meaning. Since life and death are integrated in an individual's existence, a good death is the best end of a good life.

> They [the Romans] took Rabbi Haninah ben Tradyon and wrapped a Torah scroll around him, and encompassed him with vine branches, to which they set fire. They brought woolen tufts which they soaked with water and placed over his heart, to that his soul should not depart quickly ... his disciples urged, "open your mouth that the

fire may penetrate." He replied, "better is it that the one who gave the soul should take it, than that one do oneself an injury." Then the executioner said to him, "Master, if I increase the flame and remove the woolen tufts from your heart, will you bring me to the life of the world to come?" "Yes," said Haninah … his soul departed quickly, and then the executioner threw himself into the flames.[74]

Jewish wisdom literature interprets the biblical phrase "you shall love your neighbor as yourself" as meaning "therefore, choose an easy death for him." Jewish sources absolutely prohibit any act that constitutes an obstacle to the natural process of dying. In modern terms, obstacles to death may include ventilators; they may include feeding tubes; they may include a lack of compassion, or the courage to express it, among those who surround the dying person.

7. Judaism's prohibition against suicide is ideally observed as a case of *l'hatkhilah lo, b'diavad iyn* ("in principle, no; after the fact, yes"), which is to say that simple compassion for human suffering must always temper the law. The individual's real life is not sacrificed to the abstract principle. Both the religious leader and the physician have long known this basic ethical ideal.

> "For these things I weep" (Lamentations 1:16). for Zedekiah's lack of sense and for the departure of the Presence [of G*d], said Rabbi Judah. How could Zedekiah, aware that [his children would be put to death and that then] the sadists would pierce his eyes, not have had the sense to dash his head against the wall until life left him?[75]

Death with dignity laws reassure those who are nearing death that they need not be afraid, that death can be as good and as meaningful as life. This is a profoundly beautiful expression of the Jewish law that the dying are to be considered for legal purposes *khai l'kol davar*, "like one who is alive for every purpose." Not less than human, with their choices taken away and their dignity shredded, but worthy of the same respect and capable of wielding the same power over their lives, until their very last moments, as they did in their days of health, as all of us should have the right to do at every juncture of our lives. This is what it truly means to "choose life" and to demonstrate the value of life, all the way through human life and to its end.

Jewish law respects the individual in the present moment, recognizing that it is unjust to define a person by past acts, even as it is an abdication of responsibility to rely upon precedent. This is strikingly expressed in a midrash in which the possibility is considered that Ishma'el, son of Abraham and Hagar, should have been allowed to die when he and his mother were sent away from the encampment of Abraham and Sarah. One rabbi delivers himself of the opinion that much sorrow would have been averted if the biblical father of the Arab people had not lived, and wonders why an angel was sent to save Ishma'el. Another rabbi responds that it is written in the Torah that G*d heard the child where he was, not as an adult, nor as the long-gone progenitor of an entire people, but as an innocent small child who could not possibly be considered guilty of any wrongdoing. In this way, Jewish law teaches that we must respect a person's present, personal sense of existence and its meaning, regardless of any other factors.

G*d heard the voice of the child *ba'asher hu sham,* "where he was" (Genesis 21:17). A sick person's prayer in his own behalf, where he is, is more effective than that of anyone else.[76]

ל *Lamed*
How to Die according to Jewish Ethical Teachings

This teaching is excerpted from Byron Sherwin's *Creating an Ethical Jewish Life*.

> Confronting the inevitable reality of human mortality, being conscious of individual finitude when set against the infinite plentitude of creation, causes one to pause to consider the blink of eternity that is each human life. Few

statements pose the problem as poignantly as this citation from the writings of the 17th century French philosopher Blaise Pascal:

> When I considered the short duration of my life, swallowed up in the eternity before and after, the little space which I fill, and even can see, engulfed in the infinite immensity of spaces of which I am ignorant and know me not, I am frightened, and I am astonished at being here rather than there; for there is no reason why here rather than there, why now rather than then? Who has put me here? By whose order and direction have this place and this time been allotted to me? The eternal silence of those infinite spaces frightens me.

The transient nature of human life is also keenly recognized by classical Jewish literature. For example, in the High Holiday liturgy, we read:

> The human origin is dust, and its end is dust …
> The human creature is like a clay vessel, easily broken, like withering grass, like a fading flower, Like a wandering cloud, like a fleeting breeze, like scattered dust, like an ephemeral dream.

Though death is a fact of life, there is a natural human proclivity to avoid a confrontation with one's own mortality. Both novelists and psychologists have observed that it is virtually impossible for a person to contemplate his or her own death. For example, the German author Goethe wrote, "it is entirely impossible for a thinking being to think of its own nonexistence, of the termination of its own thinking and life." Similarly, psychiatrist Karl Menninger has written, "it may be considered axiomatic that the human mind cannot conceive of its non-existence."

According to Freud, there is an intrinsic human tendency to repress death and the thought of dying.

Jewish tradition has never avoided the inevitability or the reality of death. For example, Ecclesiastes (3:1–2) forthrightly states, "A season is set for everything, a time for every experience under heaven: a time for being born, and a time for dying." Ecclesiastes (7:2) further counsels that "it is better to go to a house of mourning than into a house of feasting: for that [i.e., death] is the end of every person, and the living one should take it to heart."

The awareness of human finitude found in Hebrew Scripture is amplified in rabbinic literature. For example, the Talmud recounts that "when Rabbi Jonathan finished the book of Job, he used to say: the end of man is to die, and the end of the beast is to be slaughtered, and all are doomed to death …"

A verse in Psalms (144:4) reads," One's days are like a passing shadow." On this verse, a midrash comments: "What kind of shadow? If life is like a shadow cast by a wall, it endures … Rabbi Huna said in the name of Rabbi Aha: Life is like a bird that flies past, and its shadow flies past with it. But Samuel said: Life is like that shadow of a bee that has no substance at all."

A verse in Ecclesiastes (5:14) states, "one must depart [the world] just as one entered [the world]." On this verse, a midrash comments:

> As one enters the world so one departs. One enters with a cry and departs with a cry. One enters with tears and departs with tears. One enters in love and departs in love. One enters with a sigh and departs with a sigh. One enters devoid of knowledge and departs devoid of knowledge.

✳ It has been taught in the name of Rabbi Meir: when a person enters the world his hands are clenched as though to say: "The whole world is mine. I shall acquire it"; but when a person departs from the world his hands are spread as though to say: "I have inherited nothing from the world."

This awareness of human finitude, introduced into Judaism by the Bible and expanded upon by the Talmudic rabbis, has been incorporated into the Jewish liturgy, particularly the liturgy for the high holidays, when one is preoccupied with "who shall live and who shall die." In the *Yizkor* prayers, the memorial prayers recited on the day of atonement and on the pilgrimage festivals, it is customary to recite an excerpt from Psalm 90:

> The human is like a breath
> days are like a fleeting shadow
> In the morning flourishes
> In the evening withers away.

The deathbed confessional prayer maintains an honest, forthright attitude toward the reality of death. In this prayer, the individual does not confront death in the abstract, but the awareness of his or her own imminent departure from life:

> I acknowledge before you, Lord my G*d and G*d of my fathers, that both my cure and my death are in Your hands. May it be Your will to send me a perfect healing. Yet, if my death is determined by You, I will in love accepted at Your hand ... You who are the father of the fatherless and the judge of the widow protect my beloved kindred with whose soul my own is knit. Into Your hands

I commend my spirit. You have redeemed me, Lord G*d of Truth.

This refusal to treat death as a euphemism is discussed further in medieval Jewish religious literature. For example, Bahya ibn Pakuda wrote:

> When a person reflects on the end of his days and the speed with which his death comes, when all his hopes and wishes will cease and all his possessions will be abandoned, when he reflects on the hopelessness of retaining any of them for himself, or benefiting by them, when he imagines his condition in the grave, his face darkened, his body blackened and full of worms, its stench and putrefaction, the traces of his body all effaced, well the smell grows stronger, as if he had never washed or cleaned or exuded perfumed scents, when a man meditates upon this and matters like this, he humbles and degrades himself. He is no longer proud or arrogant …

In a similar vein, in the chapter entitled, "when one remembers, the day of death," the author of *Sefer haYashar—The Book of Righteousness*, wrote:

> It is fitting for everyone who fears the word of the Lord to reflect in his heart concerning the day of death, its calamity and its terror, and let it be to him as a reminder. Let him say in his heart, "my heart, my heart, did you not know that you were not created except to return to the dust?" From the day when you first came into being why did you not remember your final end? Do you know that all the days that you live upon the earth, you are like a passing shadow and like chaff that is

> driven away by the whirlwind from the threshing floor, and like smoke from a window. Your days are determined and your life is cut short. Every day or night that passes over you causes a lessening in the portions of your life allotted to you. Every day you draw nearer to the grave, and you will fly away without wings. Why did you not know you are dust? Why did you not remember that you were formed of the earth? ... Take hold of yourself and to be abashed and ashamed because of your sins, and give thanks to G*d while still the soul is within your body before the stars of your twilight are darkened.

While rejecting an escapist attitude for death, and advocating a frank confrontation with death and dying, Jewish tradition considers the encounter with human mortality to be an invitation neither to morbidity nor to nihilism. The attitude satirized by the prophet Isaiah (22:13), "eat, drink and be merry, for tomorrow we die," finds no place in Jewish thought. Rather, the candid awareness of human mortality is treated by Jewish religious literature as an opportunity to confront the quest for and the question of human purpose and meaning. Since life is a blind date with an uncertain future, each moment is considered a summons to begin or continue the project of creating the ultimate work of art—one's own existence. Commenting on Hillel's famous statement, "if not now, when?" a medieval Jewish writer observed that Hillel did not say, "if not *today*, when?" But "if not *now*, when?" Because "even today is in doubt regarding whether one will survive or not, for at any instant one can die." Consequently, "one cannot wait even a day or two to exert oneself in the pursuit of human fulfillment."

Attended confrontation with death can compel one to examine and to improve the moral quality of life. This notion is stated often in Talmudic literature. For example, "Rabbi Eleazar said: repent one day before your death. His disciples asked him: does then one know on what day he will die? Then all the more reason to repent today, he replied, lest he die tomorrow."

That contemplation of one's own death can serve as the ultimate guarantor of moral behavior is expressed in this Talmudic text:

> One should always incite the good impulse in his soul to fight against the evil impulse ... if he subdues it, well and good. If not, let him study the Torah ... if he subdues it, well and good. If not, let him recite the ... If he subdues it, well and good. If not, let him remind himself of the day of death ...

Reflecting on death soon after an almost fatal heart attack, the contemporary Jewish theologian, Abraham Joshua Heschel, encapsulated the Jewish attitude: "life's ultimate meaning remains obscure unless it is reflected upon in the face of death ... [Judaism's] central concern is not how to escape death but rather how to sanctify life."

Jewish responses to the problem of how to die are found in Jewish religious literature in preserved accounts of the deaths of sages, scholars, and Saints of past generations. For example, Hasidic literature contains a slim volume, *Sefer Histalkut haNefesh—The Book of the Departure of the Soul,* in which the deathbed scenes of a number of Hasidic Masters are preserved ... Without doubt, the most popularly known account of the death of the Hasidic master is the often told story of the death of Zusia of Hanipol:

> On his deathbed, Zusia began to cry. His disciples asked: "Are you crying because you are afraid that when you stand before the Holy Tribunal, they will ask you: why were you not like Moses?" "No," replied Zusia. "Then why do you weep?" The disciples asked. "Because I am afraid they will ask me why I was not like Zusia. Then what shall I say?"

> Zusia's view is paradigmatic of Jewish responses to death. Confronting death, one is led to the awesome possibility that life has not been lived to its fullness of meaning; that one has fail to realize the potentialities unique to his or her own individual self; that one has not been adequately engaged in the creation of the artful life.[77]

מ *Mem*
Tzedakah—Provisions for the Journey

> When Ukba was dying, he said, "Bring me my *tzedakah* records." He discovered that the accounts showed that he had given away seven thousand gold Sinian dinars and said, "These are small provisions for a long journey." He then gave away half his money for *tzedakah*. But how could he do that? Didn't Rabbi Ila'i say in Usha that a person should not spend more than a fifth on *tzedakah*? That rule only applies during a person's lifetime, in order to prevent the person from becoming poor, but since death makes this issue irrelevant, there is no objection.[78]

In the Jewish prayer book, there is a ritual prayer, the *El Maleh Rahamim*, which is recited four times each year according to tradition, on Yom Kippur and during the festivals of Pesakh, Shavuot, and Sukkot. In its traditional form, it specifically speaks of the *tzedakah* that the one praying promises to do in memory of the departed. In its various forms, the prayer conveys the following:

> May G*d remember the soul of _____who has gone from my sight. May memory be perpetuated through the acts of *tzedakah,* justice and generosity, that I do. May I honor the departed by upholding the ideals they lived for, and thus will that life, now gone, be present through my life's acts.

Giving to honor the memory of a dead relative or friend can be understood as an expression of hope that memory will endure.

Although we use it to denote the giving of money, *tzedakah* is literally the Hebrew for "justice." To sing as the psalmist does that *tzedakah tatzil mimavet,* "*tzedakah* saves from death," (Proverbs 10:2) is to assert that *tzedakah* staves off all that death represents: emptiness, meaninglessness, an end. Giving to support justice in all its many forms—education, liberation, peace—establishes purpose, meaning, and light. In this way, the gift of *tzedakah* is a way of lighting a candle in the darkness. Giving *tzedakah* in memory of a dead loved one directly causes that person's existence to echo for good in the world.

This ancient impulse is to keep those we have lost with us in some way through arranging to have their names spoken aloud, or at least kept visible—to keep the name alive, that the beloved dead may seem closer. It leads to wonderful acts of *tzedakah* and also to unfortunate displays of wealth. The latter were definitively addressed two thousand years ago by the wealthy Jewish leader Rabban Gamaliel, who, after he saw the way in which families competed to produce burials of their loved ones more lavish than their neighbor's, insisted on being buried in a plain wooden box—a tradition that endures to this day.

There are those who passionately believe that all *tzedakah* should be anonymous, as the great medieval scholar and jurist Maimonides taught, but there are rabbinic teachings that thoughtfully consider whether there is one correct moral stance for all times. Perhaps it is truer to say that one must carefully decide whether it is a time when anonymity is best or, rather, a time to set a graceful example.

נ *Nun*
Deathbed Teachings

There is a teaching that only those who are dying can do.

> Rabbi Eliezer was ill unto death, and his students went to visit him. They said to him, "Master, teach us the paths of life so that we may, through them, win the life of the future world." He said to them, "Be careful for the honor of your colleagues, keep your children from too much study, and expose them to scholars; and when you pray, know before whom you are standing. In this way, you will win the future world."[79]

To "win the life of the future world" may be interpreted as meriting to live again in the world to come, should there be such a world. To win the future world, though, is more clearly about the question of how one's influence in this life will echo after it.

The Torah's account of the deathbed blessing of Jacob, linked with the common human desire not to be forgotten after we die, led to an ancient Jewish tradition called the *zeva'ah*, the ethical will. In it, one recounts not one's material effects for distribution to one's heirs but the ethics one tried to live by and hopes to pass on to one's inheritors—and in this way to send an echo of yourself, what you meant by the way you lived, into the future you will not see.

On the day of the new moon in the month he was to die, the rabbi of Apt discussed at his table the death of the righteous person. When he had recited the blessing [after meals], he rose and began to walk back and forth in the room. His face glowed. Then he stopped by the table and said, "Table, pure table, you will testify on my behalf that I have properly eaten and properly taught at your board." Later, he ordered that his coffin be made out of the table.[80]

What gift might you give those who love you by speaking or writing what you've meant by the choices of your life? Is there something that needs to be said in your life? Don't let it remain unspoken. Speak of it; write it. As the great Rabbi Hillel famously asked, "If not now, when?"

Rabbi Yohanan ben Zakkai was ill unto death, and his students went to visit him … They said to him, "Master, bless us." He said to them, "May it be [G*d's] will that the fear of heaven shall be upon you like the fear of your neighbor." "His disciples said to him, "Is that all?" He said to them, "This is no small thing! You can see that when someone wants to commit a transgression, he says, 'I hope no one will see me.'"[81]

ס *Samekh*
"And Behold, Death Was Very Good"

> In the copy of Rabbi Meir's Torah was found written: "and behold, it was very [*m'od*] good" (Genesis 1:31) and also "behold, death (*mavet*) was good." Rabbi Shmuel bar Nakhman said, "I was seated on my grandfather's shoulder going up from my own town to Kfar Hana by way of Beth-Shean, and I heard Rabbi Shimon, the son of Rabbi Eleazar, say as he sat and lectured in Rabbi Meir's name: 'And behold, it was very good, and, behold, death was good.'" Rabbi Hama, the son of Rabbi Hanina and Rabbi Jonathan, said the following: "Rabbi Hama, the son of Rabbi Hanina, said: 'Adam deserved to be spared the experience of death. Why then was the penalty of death decreed against him? Because the Holy Blessed One foresaw that Nebukhadnezzar and Hiram would declare themselves G*ds; therefore was death decreed against him.'"[82]

In those days, it was common for an individual scholar and teacher such as Rabbi Meir to have his own copy of the Torah. His manuscript may have read *mavet*, "death," instead of *m'od*, "very," or he may have written it himself as a comment in a margin.

If it was not a typographical error, what did Rabbi Meir mean? Rabbi Samuel, son of Nakhman, offers evidence from his own remembered experience as a small boy, accompanying his grandfather to hear a Torah teacher who offered the interpretation that death is very good because it is a powerful impetus to repentance: in the face of death, one might turn away from much that once seemed important and see one's own behaviors in a very different light.

The first Jew had a good death:

> Abraham breathed his last, and died, satisfied, old, and full of years, and was gathered to his people.[83]

What is a "good death"? What will help us die satisfied? Each person has to discover the answer to that question. In Ecclesiastes 3:2, it is declared that death is a natural part of life: "there is a time to be born, and a time to die." Jewish tradition hints that the answer is, rightly, in our own hands.

> "A man went from the land of the Hittites and built a city. He called it Luz, and that is its name to this very day." (Judges 1:26). Concerning it we are taught that the Angel of Death has no permission to go there. When the old no longer wish to go on living, they go outside the city walls to die.[84]

ע *Ayin*
Bringing the Portrait of the King to the King

The Hasidic tale *Maaseh shel Melekh Anav, The Tale of the Humble King*, was told by Rabbi Nakhman of Bratslav:

> Once there was a king who had a wise advisor. Said the king to the wise advisor:

"There is a king who is himself mighty and great, and a man of truth and humble. He is mighty, I know he is mighty, because the sea surrounds his country, and on that sea are great ships with cannons, and they allow no one to come near. Beyond that sea there is a great swamp, and no way across it save for one narrow path, and only one person at a time can traverse it, and also there are cannons there. If anyone comes to fight, the cannons fire, and it is impossible to come near.

But how does he call himself a man of truth and humility? this I do not know. I want you to bring me a portrait of this king."

Now the king had portraits of all the kings. This king's portrait was not to be found anywhere, for he was hidden from human beings, for he sits behind a curtain, and he is far from the people of all the lands.

So the wise messenger went to this country. He knew that he would need to understand the nature of the country. How was he to learn the nature of the place? By way of the jokes. When you need to understand something, you need to learn the jokes about it. There are several kinds of jokes: there is the type in which one means to hurt someone else with one's words, and when the other objects, the first says, "I was only joking", as it is said, As a madman casts firebrands, arrows and death, so a man will deceive his neighbor and say 'I am only joking.' (Proverbs 26:18–19) And then there is one who merely seeks to laugh and even so, his companion is hurt by his words; and there are more types.

In this world of many countries there is one country that holds within it all countries of the world. In this very country there is a city that holds within it all the cities of all the countries of the world. In this very city there is a house that holds within it all the houses of all the cities of all the countries of the world. In this house there is a clown, who is the source of the jokes of all the country.

The messenger brought much wealth with him, and he went to that country, and he watched the clowning and the laughter, and he got the jokes: he understood that the country was full of lies, from beginning to end. He saw how with laughter the people cheated each other in the marketplace, and how, when he came before the magistrate, there everyone lied, and took bribes. The same was true of the authority at every level.

The messenger realized by way of this laughter that the country was full of lies and deceit, and there was no truth anyway. He went to the marketplace and was cheated, and went for judgment to the courts, and there it was the same: all lies and bribes. It's like this: today you give a bribe, and tomorrow they don't know you. He went to a higher authority, and there the same lies, until he went before the highest judicial court, and there it was the same, full of lies and bribery. And so it went until he came before the King himself.

When he came to the King, he bore witness, saying, "over whom are you king, when your country is full of lies from one end to the other? Within it there is no truth!" And he began to tell the story of all the lies of the country.

When the King heard the messenger's words, he inclined his ears toward the curtain to hear them. He wondered how it was possible that a person could be found who knew all the lies of the country. The king's ministers flew into a rage as they heard him describe the country's iniquity.

The messenger continued to testify, saying "it would be logical to assume that the King is as the country, one who loves lies like them. But rather I see that you are truly a person of truth, and that is why you are far from them, because you cannot bear the falsehoods of your country."

And the messenger began to praise the King extravagantly. Now the King really was very humble; his greatness was in his humility. This is the way of the truly humble: the more he was praised and magnified, the more he became small in his own estimation, and even more humble. As the messenger kept on heaping praises and exaltations, the King became smaller and lesser, until he became nothing at all.

No longer able to restrain himself, the King flung the curtain aside to see the messenger: Who is this who knows and understands all this? And so revealed his face.

The wise messenger saw it, and he brought his portrait to the King.

This is the end of Rabbi Nakhman's story. It leaves us with many questions. First among them is the identity of the King. In most Jewish stories, there is one King, and we understand that King to be G*d. The King in this story sends a messenger forth to get a portrait for him, but if this King is G*d, then why can't Almighty G*d see what this King looks like? And who is the King behind the curtain?

The King behind the curtain is you. You are called a "king" in this parable because you reflect the image of G*d and so manifest the presence of G*d in the world—in this country, full of lies and laughter, so far from truth.

The messenger is also you, carrying the portrait—the reflection—of you to its Source. The story has a sequel: the messenger on his way back to the King finds that no matter how much distance he travels, at the end of the day, he has not yet reached his goal. The journey back to his King, to bring the portrait of the King to the King, is a journey that will take him the rest of his life. Until the last day, that portrait is still being created, is still changing and taking shape with each word and act of your life. One day, when you yourself have become nothing at all, your portrait will be complete.

פ *Peh*
Death by a Kiss

Our masters taught: if one dies suddenly, that is "death by snatching away."

If one is sick for a day and then dies, that is "death by being hustled away." Rabbi Hananiah ben Gamaliel said that is "death by a stroke."

If one dies after two days of illness, that is "delayed death."

After three days, it is "death by reproof."

After four, it is "death by reprimand."

After five, it is "normal death as it comes to all."

If one dies before fifty, that is "premature death." At sixty, it is "death at the Hands of Heaven." At seventy, it is "death of a hoary head." At eighty, it is "death at a ripe old age." Rabbah said from fifty to sixty is "premature death."

When Rabbi Joseph turned sixty, he made a festive day for the sages, saying, "I have just passed beyond the age of premature death."

Rav Huna died suddenly. When the sages were concerned about the meaning of his death, a pair of sages from Adiabene said to them, "What we were taught concerning such a death applies only to one who has not yet reached ripe old age (eighty). After one has reached it, even sudden death is 'death by a kiss.'"[85]

Once they asked Rabbi Pinhas why, when he prayed, they could hear no sound and see no movement, so that he seemed to lack the fervor that shook the other sages from head to foot.

"Brothers," he answered, "to pray means to cling to G*d, and to cling to G*d means to lose oneself from all substance, as if the soul had left the body. Our sages say that there is a death as hard as drawing a rope through the ring on the mast, and there is a death as easy as drawing a hair out of milk, and this is called the death with a kiss. This is the one which was granted to my prayer."[86]

צ *Tzadi*
The Soul: Jewish Mystical Teachings

The soul is called by three names in the Torah, which correspond to three aspects: *nefesh,* "life force"; *ruakh,* "spirit" or "wind"; and *neshamah,* "breath." Here is how the Zohar, that great work of Jewish mysticism, describes the three aspects of your soul:

> *Nefesh,* poised to receive *nefesh* from that flowing, gushing river. *Ruakh,* presiding over it; *nefesh* is sustained only by *ruakh.* This is the *ruakh* dwelling between fire and water; from here this *nefesh* is nourished. *Ruakh* endures through the sustenance of another, higher rung, called *neshamah,* source of *nefesh* and *ruakh.* From there *ruakh* is nourished, and when *ruakh* receives, *nefesh* receives, and all is one. All draw near to one another: *nefesh* to *ruakh,* *ruakh* to *neshamah,* and all is one.[87]

The foundation of existence is at the level of *nefesh,* living being. This is the basic level of life that can be identified by the presence of breath, pulse, body warmth. The classical Jewish legal definition of life is the presence of breath. We share this *nefesh*-soul with all that lives, all that shares in the flowing river of life.

A person's *ruakh*-soul belongs to a higher level of life. In the Zohar, the mystics imagine the *ruakh* as balanced "between fire and water": between the fire of the sun and the water of the sea, between passion and calm, between surface and depths. *Ruakh* occupies a level higher than physical being; it holds emotional capacity. Like the four winds, it blows hot or cold, strong or gentle.

This *ruakh* level is the great challenge that each one of us faces in a lifetime. *Ruakh* is the emotional, passionate part of us that must balance life's stress with its serenity; its sadness with its joy; its angers, frustrations, and violence with its happiness, contentment, and calm. Every day, we are confronted with the need to balance between who we mean to be and who we are; what we mean to say and what we utter; what we ought to have done and what we did. *Ruakh* experiences all the storms and upheavals of the human heart, tossed about this way and that by every passing desire.

The highest level of soul is *neshamah*; this is the breath-soul, and we find it associated with understanding by the mystics. This is the cool, quiet place after the storms of the heart. It is not a place devoid of emotion, not at all; mercy dwells here, and compassion for all that the heart helplessly suffers. The *neshamah* is the place of redemption, where you are freed from the heart's rule over you. You are able, when dwelling in the *neshamah* soul, to understand, to forgive, to find yourself responding to the world with compassion. This is the deepest and highest, most rarified part of the soul. This soul links upper to lower; it is the source and support of *ruakh* and *nefesh*. With it, one is able to leave Egypt—that place of narrow straits we all know in life, a personal Egypt of our own particular enslavement.

Somehow, all three of these levels become one in a life. Indeed, this is the work of a life: to become one, a whole person. In order to do this, we must clear the channels between heart and mind, not only our own but also the channels between us—and not only in this moment of time but across generations and geography.

Egypt is the inevitable place where we find ourselves after a lifetime of mistakes and regrets, and it is only in the effort to become whole that we redeem ourselves from there. You leave Egypt by making atonement with those you have wronged, by speaking the words someone is waiting to hear spoken. In atonement, you find, finally, at-one-ment and the serenity of being all right with the world. At one, at peace, and at home.

> "The divine One knows that we will die," said Rabbi Eliezer. "Why are souls sent into the world by G*d's will? Why does G*d need them?" he asked Rabbi Shimon.
>
> "Many have asked for wisdom on this question," came the answer. "The souls descend into the world to reflect the radiance of the divine. Then, they ascend once again.
>
> "Here is the mystery: when the soul ascends, the female's desire for the male is awakened. A cleaving follows, and the connection between upper and lower worlds is perfected through this union. The just and ascending soul arouses desire above when it rises, leading toward the time when all is united through the divine union of the highest spheres."[88]

G*d seeks a unification with the world that cannot be achieved without the longing of the human soul, trapped in the vessel of its earthly body, for its Source. In our own lives, we know the loneliness of dwelling inside the envelope of skin that separates us from each other and from the all to which we belong. When we act toward the unification of our own disparate parts, becoming a more whole self by linking our highest ideals with our most foundational existence, we create a small version of that bridge between heaven and earth. When we link the transcendent and the imminent within ourselves, we bring all of existence—all of G*d—one step closer to that oneness.

The mystics sensed that in such a way we draw closer to G*d, returning to our Source as a spark returns to a fire, or a drop of water returns to the ocean. That moment of reunification with G*d is, of course, the end of separate human existence. Does the drop of water exist when it merges with the sea? That becoming one with G*d means the end of the individual seemed for the mystics the most wonderful kind of death possible.

> For a number of hours Rabbi Uri lay unconscious in the agony of death. His favorite disciple, Rabbi Yehudah Zevi, opened the door from time to time, looked at the dying man, and closed the door again. At last he entered the room and went up to the bed. The next moment the students who had followed him in saw their master stretch out one last time, and die. Later, when they asked Rabbi Yehudah how he had known that death was imminent, he replied, "It is written: 'For man shall not see Me and live.' I saw that he saw."[89]

ק *Kuf*
The Mourner's *Kaddish*

This is a poetic translation of the *Kaddish Yatom*, the Mourner's *Kaddish*, a prayer which is traditionally recited in memory of the dead by their family and descendants. It is recited only in the presence of a minyan of ten Jews, an ancient ritual requirement expressing an eternal truth—that no one should grieve alone.

The prayer itself does not mention death. Rather it asserts praise of G*d, the giver of life, even in the face of death.

> May we find a way to praise G*d who is above all praise;
> may G*d's presence be a comforting reality in every heart.

> G*d is blessed, praised, glorified, exalted, magnified,
> a holiness awesome and above and beyond all understanding,
> beyond all words.

> May our lives be blessed by this awareness that we are not alone;
> there is a Source of Life and Love and Meaning for our lives.

> May the One who makes peace up there,
> in mercy make peace for us down here, Amen!
>
> May all who mourn know the peace of Wholeness,
> may all who are bereaved find consolation through us,
> and let us together say
>
> Amen.

ר *Reysh*
Not Wanting to Die: The Death of Moses

This is an excerpt from an ancient and very long account of the death of Moses:

> G*d said unto Moses, "Behold, your days approach that you must die" (Deuteronomy 31:14). These words are to be considered in the light of the verse "Though his excellency rise up to the heavens, and his head reach unto the clouds, yet he shall perish … They that have seen him shall say 'where is he?'" (Job 20:6–7). To whom does this verse refer? To none other than [to one who nears] the day of death. Even if one would make oneself wings like a bird and go up to heaven, once the time comes to die, the wings will be broken and one falls down.
>
> The words "though his excellency rise up to the heavens" apply particularly to Moses, who went up to heaven, whose feet stood on thick clouds, who became like the ministering angels, who spoke with the Holy One face to face, who received the Torah from G*d's own hand—yet when his time came, the Holy One said, "Behold your days approach that you must die."
>
> When Moses realized that the decree [of death] had been sealed against him, he drew a small circle around himself, stood in it, and said, "Master of the Universe, I will not

budge from here until You void that decree." At the same time, he donned sackcloth—indeed, wrapped himself in it—strewed ashes upon himself, and persisted in prayer and supplications before the Holy One, until heaven and earth—indeed, all things made during the six days of creation—were shaken, so that they said, "Perhaps the intention of the Holy One to remake the World is about to be executed." A divine voice came forth and said, "As yet, the Holy One's intention to remake the World is not about to be executed. But the words 'in whose hand is the soul of every living thing' (Job 12:10) [are in force and apply even to Moses]."

…

Moses said to the Holy One, "Master of the Universe, known and revealed to You is the trouble and pain I suffered on account of Israel, until they came to believe in You. How much pain I suffered because of them, until I inculcated among them the Torah and its precepts! I said to myself: As I witnessed their woe, so will I be allowed to witness their weal. Yet now that Israel's weal has come, You tell me, "you shall not go over this Jordan (Deuteronomy 24:15). You manifestly turn into fraud. Is such the reward for forty years that I labored until Israel became a holy people loyal to their faith?" The Holy One replied, "Nevertheless, such is the decree that has gone forth from My Presence." Then Moses said. "Master of the Universe, if I am not to enter the Land alive, let me enter dead, as the bones of Joseph are about to enter." The Holy One replied, "Moses, when Joseph came to Egypt, he did not deny his identity. He declared openly, 'I am a Hebrew.' But when you came to Midian, you denied yours."

Then Moses said, "Master of the Universe, if You will not let me enter the Land of Israel, allow me to remain [alive] like the beasts of the field, who eat grass, drink water, and thus savor the world – let me be like one of these." At that, G*d replied, "enough. Speak no more to Me of this matter" (Deuteronomy 3:26).

But Moses spoke up again, "Master of the Universe, if not [like a beast of the field], then let me become like a bird that flies daily in every direction to gather its food and in the evening returns to its nest—let me be like one of these." The Holy One replied again, "Enough."

When Moses saw that his prayer was not heeded, he went to implore heaven and earth …
He went to the sun and the moon …
He went to implore the stars and the planets …
Then he went to implore the mountains and the hills …

Then he went to implore the sea and cried: Entreat mercy on my behalf. The sea replied, Son of Amram, why is this day different from former days? Are you not the same son of Amram who came to me with your rod, smote me, split me into twelve paths, when I could not withstand you because the Presence was proceeding at your right? What's happened to you now? As the sea reminded Moses of what he was able to do in his younger years, he cried out in anguish, "Oh that I were as in the months of old" (Job 29:2).

…

Moses said to G*d, Master of the Universe, shall the feet that went up to the firmament, the face that confronted the Presence, the hands that received the Torah from Your hand—shall these now lick dust?

The Holy One replied: Such was My thought [from the very beginning], and such must be the way of the world: each generation is to have its own interpreters of Scripture, each generation is to have its own providers, each generation is to have its own leaders.

…

The Holy One said to Gabriel: Go forth and bring the soul of Moses. Gabriel replied: He who is equal in importance to sixty myriads—how can I bear to watch him dying?

Then the Holy One said to Michael: Go and bring the soul of Moses. Michael replied: I was his teacher, and he my pupil. How can I bear to watch him dying?

Then the Holy One said to Sama'el: Go and fetch the soul of Moses … he immediately clothed himself with anger, girded on his sword, wrapped himself in ruthlessness, and went forth to encounter Moses. Sama'el found him seated and writing the Ineffable Name on a scroll. The radiance of his appearance was like the radiance of the sun's visage; indeed, Moses looked like an angel of the Lord of Hosts.

Sama'el was so frightened by the sight of Moses that trembling seized him, so that he found himself unable to open his mouth to say anything, until Moses asked Sama'el, "Evil one, what are you doing here?" "I have come to take away your soul." "Who sent you?" "The One who created all beings." "Go away. I want to praise the Holy One—'I shall not die but live, and declare the works of G*d'" (Psalm 118:17).

…

A divine voice came forth and said, "The time has come for you to depart the world." Moses pleaded with the Holy One, "Master of the Universe, for my sake, remember the time when I stood on Mount Sinai for forty days and forty nights. I beg You, do not hand me over to the angel of death."

Again a divine voice came forth and said, "Fear not, I Myself will attend you and your burial."

Moses pleaded, "Then wait until I bless Israel. One account of the warnings and reprimands I heaped upon them, they never found any ease with me." Then he began to bless each tribe separately, but when he saw that time was running short, he included all the tribes in a single blessing.

Then he said to Israel, "Because of the Torah and its precepts, I troubled you greatly. Now, please forgive me."

They replied, "Our master, our lord, you are forgiven." In their turn they said to him, "Moses our teacher, we troubled you even more, we made your burden so heavy. Please forgive us." Moses replied, "you are forgiven."

Again a divine voice came forth: "The moment has come for you to depart from this world." Moses replied, "Blessed be the Name, may it live and endure forever and ever!" Then he said to Israel, "I implore you, when you enter the Land, remember me and my bones, and say 'Alas for the son of Amram, who had run before us like a horse, yet his bones fell in the wilderness.'"

Again a divine voice came forth and said, "Within half a moment you are to depart from the world."

Moses lifted both his arms, placed them over his heart, and called out to Israel, "Behold the end of flesh and blood." … Then, from the highest heaven of heavens, the Holy One came down to take the soul of Moses, and with G*d the ministering angels, Michael, Gabriel, and

Zagzagel. Michael laid out his bier, Gabriel spread a fine linen cloth at his head, while Zagzagel spread it as his feet. Michael stood at one side and Gabriel at the other. Then the Holy One said to Moses, "Moses, close your eyes," and he closed his eyes. "Put your arms over your breast," and he put his arms over his breast. "Bring your legs together," and be brought his legs together. Then the Holy One summoned Moses' soul, saying, "My daughter, I had fixed the time of your sojourn in the body of Moses at a hundred and twenty years. Now your time has come to depart. Depart. Delay not."

She replied, "Master of the Universe, I know that You are G*d of all spirits and Lord of all souls. You created me and placed me in the body of Moses one hundred and twenty years ago. Is there a body in the world more pure than the body of Moses? I love him, and I do not wish to depart from him."

The Holy One exclaimed, "depart, and I will take you up to the highest heaven of heavens, and will set you under the Throne of Glory, next to the cherubim and seraphim."

In that instant, the Holy One kissed Moses, and took his soul with that kiss.

At that, the *Shekhinah* wept and said, "A prophet has never since arisen in Israel like Moses" (Deuteronomy 34:10).

The heavens wept and said, "A good man has perished from the earth" (Micah 7:2).

The earth wept and said, "And the upright among men is no more" (Micah 7:2).

The ministering angels wept and said, "He did G*d's righteousness" (Deuteronomy 33:21).

Israel wept and said, "And G*d's judgments with Israel" (Deuteronomy 33:21).

They all said together, "May he enter in peace and rest in peace" (Isaiah 57:2).⁹⁰

ש *Shin*
Dying as a Jew

Abraham gave all that he had to Isaac. To his other children Abraham gave gifts, and he sent them away from Isaac while he yet lived, eastward. And these are the days of the years of Abraham's life which he lived, a hundred and seventy-five years. Abraham expired and died in a good old age, an old man sated with years; and he was gathered to his people. His sons Isaac and Ishmael buried him in the cave of Makhpelah, in the field of Ephron son of Zohar the Hittite, which is near Mamre; the field which Abraham purchased of the Hittite people; there Abraham was buried alongside Sarah his wife. And it was after the death of Abraham that God blessed Isaac his son; and Isaac lived by The Well of the Living G*d. (Genesis 25:5–11)

Moses went from the plains of Moab up Mt Nebo, to the top of Pisgah, over against Jerikho. G*d showed him all the land, even Gilead as far as Dan; and all Naphtali, and the land of Ephraim and Manasseh, and all the land of Judah as far as the last Sea; and the Negev, and the Plains even the valley of Jerikho, that city of palm-trees, as far as Zoar. G*d said to him: 'This is the land which I swore to Abraham, to Isaac, and to Jacob, saying: I will give it unto your descendants; I have caused you to see it with your own eyes, but you will not go over there.' So Moses the servant of G*d died there in the land of Moab, at the mouth of G*d. He was buried in the valley in the land of

Moab over against Beth-peor; no one knows where unto this day. (Deuteronomy 34:1–6)

It has been the custom in some places for people to be buried in coffins that were made from the tables upon which they studied, or upon which they fed the poor, or upon which they worked faithfully at their trade. (*Kav haYashar* 46)

Six voices go from one end of the world to the other and the sound is not audible. ... When a fruit-bearing tree is cut down the voice cries out from one end of the world to the other, and its sound is not audible. ... When the soul departs from the body the voice goes out from one end of the world to the other, and its sound is not audible. (*Pirke d'Rabbi Eliezer* 34)

ת *Tahv*
G*d Is the *Mikveh* of Israel

The Hebrew word *mikveh*, "gathering of waters," can also be translated "hope." The Gerer Rebbe taught:

> The Sages said "G*d is the hope [*mikveh*] of Israel" (Jeremiah 17:13)—just as a *mikveh* prepares the one who transitions, so does the blessed Holy One prepare Israel. Just as one enters the *mikveh's* waters with all one's being, so does one plunge one's entire self into nothingness in G*d.
>
> It is a great privilege when one dies, to experience this transition in the *mikveh*, the Hope, of the blessed Holy One.[91]

Endnotes to Volume 1: *The Alef Bet of Death*

All Zohar translations are taken from Daniel Matt, translator, Zohar: Pritzker Edition (Stanford University Press, 2006).

BT refers to the Babylonian Talmud.

A special Todah Rabah to author, teacher, and mensch Danny Siegel, from whom I had the privilege to learn when just beginning my Torah study journey and whose three-volume *Where Heaven and Earth Touch* has accompanied me all my days as a rabbi. His teachings and his choice of texts breathe through this work.

1   Hasidic saying taught by Dr. Louis Jacobs ז״ל to Dr. Byron Sherwin ז״ל, related to the author in a private conversation.
2   Mishle 20:27.
3   Bereshit 2:7.
4   Kohelet 12:7.
5   Tehilim 65:2.
6   Yalkut Shimoni on Bereshit 1:3.
7   Kohelet Rabbah 3:2–3.
8   Tehilim 23:4.
9   Moshe Isserles, commentary to Shulkhan Arukh, Yoreh Deah 339:1.
10 *Arba'ah Turim, Darkhei Moshe*, 339:1.
11 Rabbi Yehudah Leib Alter of Ger, *Likkutei Sefat Emet, Va'Era* 2.
12 Rabbi Kalonymos Kalmish Shapira, *Sacred Fire*, trans. J. Hershy Worch (Rowman & Littlefield, 2000), 210–211.
13 Rabbi Issakhar of Zlotchov, cited by Dr. Yehudah Gellman, Shalom Hartman Institute, spring 2002.
14 Yosef Hayim Yerushalmi, *Zakhor: Jewish History and Jewish Memory* (Seattle: University of Washington Press, 1983), 10.
15 *Midrash Rabbah, VaYekhi* 5.
16 Consult with a qualified rabbi for other types of gender identification.
17 *BaMidbar* 19:11–13.
18 Zohar 1:32a.

19 See, for example, the collection of legends in "Travelers' Tales" in *The Book of Legends,* eds. Hayim Nahman Bialik and Yehoshua Hana Ravnitsky, trans. William Braude (Shocken, 1992), 784–785.
20 Zohar I, 98a, cited in Isaac Tishby, *Wisdom of the Zohar,* volume 2 (Littman Library, 1991), 833.
21 From the last verse of "Adon Olam," a song found in the Jewish prayer book. It is considered of ancient but uncertain authorship. There is a tradition in some places to recite it on one's deathbed.
22 Bereshit [Genesis] 25:7–10.
23 Bereshit [Genesis] 24:1.
24 Zohar 1:224b.
25 BT Berakhot 31a.
26 Pirke Avot 6:9.
27 Bereshit [Genesis] 49:1–2.
28 Bereshit [Genesis] 49:18.
29 *Mei haShiloakh* commentary on *Bereshit Rabbah* 98:1, in Aviva Gottlieb Zornberg, *The Murmuring Deep* (Schocken, 2009), 338.
30 *Tehilim* [Psalm] 34:13–15.
31 BT *Berakhot* 34b.
32 Elliot R Wolfson, *The Book of the Pomegranate: Moses de Leon's Sefer ha-Rimmon* (Scholar's Press, 1988), 181–182.
33 *Bereshit* [Genesis] 2:7.
34 Maimonides, "Death through the Kiss of G*d," *The Guide for the Perplexed,* trans. M. Friedlander (1956), 390–391.
35 *Siddur Shir Tikvah,* translator Miles Hochstein (Congregation Shir Tikvah, Portland, OR, 2013), 56.
36 *Bereshit* [Genesis] 1:27.
37 BT *Shabbat* 133b.
38 *Tehilim* [Psalm] 90:12.
39 *VaYikra* [Leviticus] 19:2.
40 Literally "first"; this is a reference to the *sefirot,* a mystical description of G*d's ten attributes or characteristics, first of which is *Hokhmah,* wisdom.
41 *Degel Mahaneh Ephraim, parashat Kedoshim* (Warsaw, 1883), 104.
42 Isaiah 6:3.
43 Study house.
44 "The Besht and the Angel of Death," in Dan Ben-Amos and Jerome R. Mintz, *In Praise of the Baal Shem Tov - Shivkhei Ha-Besht: the Earliest Collections of Legends about the Founder of Hasidism* (Jason Aronson, Inc., 1976), 116.
45 *Yelammedenu* in Yalkut Proverbs, 943.
46 "Nakhman of Bratslav," trans. Aryeh Kaplan, in Perle Besserman, *Teachings of the Jewish Mystics* (Shambhala, 1998), 103.

47 Robert Alter, *Psalms* (W.W. Norton & Company, 2009), 321–322, excerpted and adapted.

Citations in Boxes

"Rava said to Rav Nakhman," BT *Mo'ed Katan* 28a.
"Against your will," *Yalkut Shimoni* on *Bereshit* 1:3.
"When Rabbi Bunem," Martin Buber, *Tales of the Hasidim*, volume 2 (New York, Schoken, 1947), 268.
"My heart says" *Tehillim* [Psalms] 27:8
"We do not need," BT *Shekalim* 2:5.
"The time drew near," *Bereshit* [Genesis[47.29.
"Rav Sheshet," BT *Mo'ed Katan* 28a.
"Rabbi Yossi," BT *Shabbat* 118b.
"G*d You are the strength," Lawrence Kushner and Nehemiah Polen, *Filling Words with Light: Hasidic and Mystical Perspectives on Jewish Prayer* (Jewish Lights Publishing, 2007), 120-121.
"One who brings joy," Maimonides, *Mishneh Torah* Laws of *Megillah* 2.16-17 cited in Danny Siegel, *Where Heaven and Earth Touch,* volume 2 (Town House Press, 1984), 14.
"One who does not approach," Martin Buber, *Hasidism and Modern Man* (1957; Princeton University Press reprint 2016), 15.

Endnotes to Volume 2: *Dying as a Jew*

48 Abraham Joshua Heschel, "Death as Homecoming" in *Jewish Reflections on Death*, ed. Jack Riemer (Schocken, 1974), 58.
49 See, for example, the *Gevurah* prayer, second of the prayers of the *Amidah*.
50 "The Story of the Humble King," a parable of Rabbi Nakhman of Bratslav, author's translation.
51 *Bereshit Rabbah* 10.
52 BT *Avodah Zarah* 17a.
53 BT *Yoma* 85b.
54 Isaiah Tishby, *The Wisdom of the Zohar*, volume 2 (1949; 1989), 833.
55 Rabbi Hayim Pelaggi, *Hikkeke Leb* I, 50:190a–191a, in "A Prayer To Hasten Death," *A Treasury of Responsa*, trans. Solomon Freehof (1960), 220–223.
56 Louis Jacobs, "Theological Responsa," in *Judaism*, (summer 1967), excerpted.
57 Translations of the *Book of Jonah* from Sefaria.org open source: Modernized Tanakh—based on Jewish Publication Society 1917, edited by Adam Cohen.
58 Author's translation.
59 *BaMidbar* (Numbers), literally "in the wilderness": chapter 20, verses 1–2. In the first month, the entire Israelite community came to the Zin Desert, and the people stopped in Kadesh. It was there that Miriam died and was buried. The people did not have any water, and they began demonstrating against Moses and Aaron.
60 "Miriam died." Some say that she died on 1 Nissan (*Seder Olam* 9; *Midrash HaGadol*; Josephus, Antiquities 4:4:6), while others say that she died on 10 Nisan (*Megillath Taanith* 13; *Targum Yonathan*; *Orach Hayim* 580:2). Some say that the Israelites arrived in Kadesh on 1 Nissan and Miriam died on 10 Nisan (*Shalshelet HaKabbalah; Seder HaDorot*). It was about the same time that the message was sent to the king of Edom (*Seder Olam* 9). Josephus, however, has the encounter with Edom before Miriam's death (Antiquities 4:4:5).
61 "Miriam died there." RASHI (Rabbi Shlomo Yitzhaki): She too died with a (divine) kiss. And why is it not stated regarding her, *al pi Adonai*, "by the mouth of the Eternal"? *She'ayno derekh kavod shel ma'alah*, because it is not a respectful [attitude to take] toward the Most High. But regarding Aaron, it is stated, "by the mouth of the Eternal" in *BaMidbar* [Numbers] 33:38.
62 "The Angel," from *Niddah* 30b, *Seder Yetzirat haVelad*, trans. Danny Siegel. *Where Heaven and Earth Touch*, volume 1 (New York: Townhouse Press, 1983), 20–22, used with permission.
63 Alice Walker, *The Temple of My Familiar* (Open Road, 2011).
64 See *Ayin* in this volume.

65 *Tanhuma, Mishpatim* 12.
66 BT *Semakhot* 9.
67 BT *Ketubot* 46b.
68 Miriam Schneider and Jan Selliken Bernard, *Midwives to the Dying* (Angels' Work, 1992), 8–11.
69 *Yalkut, Hukkat* 764.
70 J. David Bleich, "The Quinlan Case" in *Jewish Bioethics,* ed. Rosner et al. (Ktav, 2000), 36.
71 Maimonides, *Mishneh Torah,* "Fundamentals of the Torah" 5.4,10, ed. Birnbaum (Hebrew Publishing Company, 1944, 1974), 8–9.
72 *Yelammedenu* in *Yalkut, Proverbs,* 943.
73 BT *Shabbat* 31a.
74 BT *Avodah Zarah* 18a.
75 *Eikhah Rabbah* 1:16, 51.
76 *Bereshit Rabbah* 53:14.
77 "How to Die," Byron Sherwin (excerpted), *Creating an Ethical Jewish Life* (Jewish Lights, 2001), used by permission of the estate.
78 BT *Ketubot* 67b.
79 BT *Berakhot* 28b.
80 Martin Buber, "The Table" in *Tales of the Hasidim,* volume 2 (New York: Schocken, 1947).
81 BT *Berakhot* 28b.
82 *Bereshit Rabbah* 9:5.
83 *Bereshit* [Genesis] 25:8.
84 BT *Sotah* 46b.
85 BT *Mo'ed Katan* 28a.
86 Martin Buber, "The Easy Death" in *Tales of the Hasidim,* volume 1 (New York: Schocken, 1947).
87 *Zohar* 1:206a, trans. Daniel Matt, Zohar Pritzker edition, volume 3 (Stanford, 2006), 263–264.
88 *Zohar* 1.235a, trans. David Rosenberg, *Dreams of Being Eaten Alive* (Harmony Books, 2000), 110–111.
89 Martin Buber, "The Sign" in *Tales of the Hasidim,* volume 2 (New York: Schocken, 1947).
90 Eds. Hayim Nakhman Bialik and Yehoshua Hana Ravnitsky, "The Death of Moses" in *The Book of Legends: Sefer HaAggadah—Legends from the Talmud and Midrash,* trans. William Braude (Schocken, 1992), 101–104, excerpted.
91 "Yom Kippur 2," 5:170, Rabbi Yehudah Leib Alter of Ger *Sefer Sfat Emet,* ed. Shai Gloskin (Jewish Publication Society, 1998), 103.

CPSIA information can be obtained
at www.ICGtesting.com
Printed in the USA
LVHW102147090522
718368LV00001B/2